KU-600-749

METHUEN
HANDBOOK OF ROSES

METHUEN
HANDBOOK OF
ROSES

BY EIGIL KIAER

WITH ILLUSTRATIONS BY
VERNER HANCKE

TRANSLATED BY GWYNNE VEVERS

WITH ADDITIONAL MATERIAL BY
FRED FAIRBROTHER, M.SC., F.R.I.C.
Past President of the Royal National Rose Society

LONDON
METHUEN & CO LTD

First published by Politikens Forlag, Denmark, in 1965
as Den Store Rosenbog
Copyright in all countries signatory to the Berne Convention
English translation first published in Great Britain, 1966
by Methuen & Co. Ltd, 11 New Fetter Lane, London EC4
© *1966 by Methuen & Co. Ltd, London and*
E. P. Dutton & Co. Inc., New York
Colour plates printed in Holland by Ysel Press, Deventer
Text printed in Great Britain by John Dickens & Co. Ltd, Northampton

Contents

Dedicated to
Svend Poulsen and his wife

Foreword

The production of garden roses is increasing year by year, and interest in them has probably never been so great as it is at the present time. This, together with a desire to increase interest in roses among owners of private gardens has been a major reason for the publication of this Handbook of Roses.

To create a book which provides practical information for the gardener together with a collection of attractive illustrations for the rose enthusiast has proved to be an arduous task. It has taken three years for the original idea to develop through its various stages. The selection of varieties took a long time, and the process of completing the illustrations and perfecting the reproduction of the plates was delayed by the seasons – for all of Verner Hancke's coloured plates were painted from typical and perfect specimens of cut roses; the artist's work, therefore was limited to the period when the varieties were in bloom.

The most modern methods available have been employed to reproduce the original paintings, and this involved close cooperation between the artist and the lithographer.

Professor Asger Klougart, Niels Poulsen, the nurseryman, and Harry Hansen, the consultant, have all helped to produce the book as it now stands; it is a book not only of roses but also a handbook, containing practical instructions and guidance which should be of use to all who are interested in gardening.

The selection of varieties is certainly one of the largest hitherto illustrated in colour for a book of roses, and I would like to express my gratitude to the specialists within the rose industry who gave valuable advice in the difficult task of selection, and who supported the project in many other ways.

First and foremost I should like to thank Denmark's finest rose expert, O. Sønderhousen who read the proofs for rose nomenclature and who also gave generous help in other matters. I should also like to thank the great rose-breeder, Dr Svend Poulsen, who over a generation has taught me so much of the noble art of growing roses.

Many of the beautiful roses were painted from cut flowers in the large new rose garden in Valby Park, Copenhagen, and in the rose garden of the Agricultural College, Copenhagen. In this connection, I would like to express my thanks to the Copenhagen City gardener, Mr Jacob Bergmann, and to Professor Asger Klougart of the Agricultural College.

Harold Nielsen, the pharmacist, readily placed his extensive knowledge of the cultural history of these plants at the disposal of the editor; this has been of special value in the first part of the book.

Many new varieties will doubtless arise during the coming years – indeed, several beautiful and valuable varieties have already appeared since the original selection was made; some of these merit a place among the colour plates, and it is hoped that it will be possible to prepare a new edition so that a place can be found for them.

The rose is undoubtedly the most popular flower in our gardens, but it is not easy to say why this should be so. Perhaps it is worth turning first to the history of the rose in search of an explanation.

The rose is one of the few flowers which has been associated with mankind throughout the ages – it has found a place in religion, in love, in war and in literature. A survey of this long, fascinating association and the ways in which the various links have been forged is provided by the historical illustrations and text of the first section of the book. The influence of the rose on art, literature, architecture and indeed on all aspects of human life is examined here – with the conclusion that no other flower can approach the unique position of the rose in relation to mankind. Here, I believe, lies the explanation of why this flower means so much to so many people today.

EIGIL KIAER

The cultural history of the rose

Now and again one hears sceptical voices warning against the planting of too many roses, on the grounds that they take too much space which would be better used for the cultivation of fruit and vegetables. Such earnest words of wisdom have been heard for many years – two thousand years ago Horace was complaining about the state of affairs in the Roman state, where wheatfields and orchards were being planted with roses.

The rose has been present in all the periods of man's prosperity and has played an important role in history, religion, poetry, in politics and economics. Its role in advertising has always been evocative of something sublime. Moreover, it was first chosen as the Queen of the Flowers thousands of years ago. Reference to this poetic choice was made by the Greek writer, Achilles Tatius (ca. 450 A.D.), who quotes the following lines; it is just possible that they were written by Sappho, the poetess, who lived a thousand years before Tatius.

> "If Zeus has willed it so
> That o'er the flowers one flower should reign a
> queen,
> I know, ah well I know
> The rose, the rose, that royal flower had been!
> She is of earth the gem,
> Of flowers the diadem
> And with her flush
> The meadows blush."

Our information on very early times is only fragmentary, and a pattern is only apparent to

9

those who use their imagination. Nevertheless, it can be stated quite clearly that the history of man and of the rose have been linked together for some 5000 years.

Roses have naturally been influenced by this close association with man. Their appearance has changed over the ages and has been affected by the locality in which they were grown and by the purpose which they served. Roses have always proved to be readily adaptable, and since ancient times, they have been praised both in art and in literature.

ANCIENT TIMES

Before man began to experiment with the products of nature, roses were found only in places where the environment was naturally suited to them; species were then decided by climate and soil.

Originally, there were about 120 known wild species distributed over the northern hemisphere with two particular centres, one in central Asia, the other in western Europe.

Each of these main areas branched out into diverging species. These had certain characteristics in common: they were thorny plants with pinnate leaves, a flower with five petals and a fleshy fruit with hard seeds.

The difference between the species in the east and those in the west lay in the cell nuclei of the plants. These were hidden barriers to the mixing of races. No one knew of the existence of the varying chromosome numbers which regulated and restricted these possibilities.

Asia is the place of origin of the most beautiful species, and from there they were brought to the Near East, perhaps principally on account of the fruit's nutritious and medicinal value.

As man encroaches on nature, he brings strange species into the environment of his houses and towns. These species interbreed and hybrid vigour arises from the plant's modest hereditary material. This development of hybrid vigour does not take place quickly, but occurs gradually, step by step, influenced by the development of human culture which is inevitably a slow growth of new ideas.

Rosa provincialis major.   Rosa gallica.   Rosa alba.

Woodcuts from Neu vollkommen Kräuterbuch, *1687, by D. Jacobus Theodorus Tabernaemontanus, except* R. gallica *which is from* Kreuterbuch, *1679, by Adamus Lonicerus.*

ARCHAEOLOGICAL EVIDENCE

The archaeologists provide us with our first knowledge of the rose side by side with man. It was Sir Leonard Woolley, who found the famous royal groves of Ur in Chaldaea, in the Euphrates–Tigris region, and who showed, amongst other things, that the Sumerian King Sargon (2648–2630 B.C.) returned from a campaign bringing "vines, figs and roses to his country". That was some 5000 years ago!

After this discovery, there is an immense gap in our knowledge. We must, however, assume that roses were first brought to Crete and Greece by road. Caravans also wandered from the rivers of Babylonia, taking their culture with them right across Egypt to north Africa.

Extremely little is known about roses in the Egypt of the Pharaohs. There is scarcely any evidence of them before about 300 B.C. In 1888, a small wreath with nine roses embossed on it was found in an Egyptian grave from about 400–200 B.C. This was what the Romans later named *Rosa sancta* – a variety of *R. gallica*, which the Egyptians are supposed to have obtained from the Hebrews.

The Bible mentions the Rose of Sharon; Isaiah, chap. 35 reads "and the desert shall rejoice and blossom as the rose". There has been doubt about whether the translators picked on the correct flower name; but it is thought that Babylonia had several species of rose, which were collected from Persia, a country known for its wealth of these plants. The holy script of the Persians, the *Avasta* – which forms the basis of one of the world's oldest religions – used the rose as a religious symbol. Furthermore, archaeological finds suggest that the rose had been cultivated in Palestine before the birth of Christ.

Remains of a rose cult have been found both in India and in Syria – and a rose is stamped on one of the oldest coins which has been unearthed in the Middle East.

FLOWER OF APHRODITE

The oldest pictures of roses on ornaments come from Crete (about 1600 B.C.). But with their six petals, these are scarcely correct botanically.

A silver 2-drachma coin from Rhodes, ca. 80 B.C. The rose motif was often used on the island, which was the main seat of the cult of Helios. It is thought that the rose represents the island's name-giver, who was the mistress of Helios.

At this period of history, man began to praise the rose in poetry and prose; it was honoured and worshipped, and it played a role in various cults.

Homer (ca. 900 B.C.) wrote that the "shield of Achilles was decorated with roses", and that "Aphrodite embalmed Hector's body with rose compounds". The rose became consecrated to Aphrodite, the goddess of beauty and love, and later to Eros.

The rose was also a symbol in mythology and the Greek poet Anachreon (ca. 600 B.C.), who often sang about it, said that the rose grew from the white foam that covers Aphrodite when she rises up out of the sea. In his fifth ode, the rose is the subject of special homage:

> *"The season that to man hath sent*
> *The rose, that sweetest ornament,*
> *Pray duplicate in silver line*
> *to make my drinking sweet and fine."*
> Translated by J. M. Edmonds in
> *Elegy and Iambus*, vol. 2, 1931 (Heinemann).

Another song also told of Aphrodite who allowed red roses to grow out from the blood of her beloved Adonis after he had been torn asunder by a wild boar.

There are various other legends about the rose –

Part of a Chinese silk painting by Chan Ching-feng. The painting dates from the sixteenth century – during the Ming dynasty – long before Chinese roses had reached Europe. It was not until the end of the eighteenth century that the western world learned about the beautiful roses of eastern Asia, including R. chinensis and R. chinensis semperflorens.

including the one which tells of the beautiful young queen, Rhodanthe, from Corinth who changed into a rose when her admirers became too importunate.

AND SO THE CULT OF THE ROSE SPREADS
It is not known when the rose came to Greece. The oldest writers name the island of Kithira as the domicile of the rose, and at the same time this island was renowned for its cult of Venus. The historian, Herodotus, was of the opinion that the famous King Midas had brought the rose with

him from Asia Minor when he moved to Macedonia in about 700 B.C.; in this connection, he describes a rose with 60 petals. However, the first real description of a rose is given by the naturalist, Theophrastus, who died in 285 B.C.

The cult of roses spread over the whole of ancient Greece, and the custom, which is still known today, of strewing roses on graves can be traced back to this period. In ancient writings, one can see that there was no more desirable offering on a grave than rose blooms and rose wreaths.

About the same time, Greek colonists took the rose to south Italy, Sicily, and north Africa. From south Italy, it extended to Campania and thence to the whole of the Italian peninsula. It spread further to Spain, France and possibly, even at this early period, to England.

THE ROSE IN CHINA
Turning now to China, we find that roses occupied a place of honour in this very ancient state, where so many of our other important cultivated plants originated. The philosopher Confucius (551–479 B.C.) states that in his time there were 600 books on roses in the library of the Chinese Emperor. They knew about rose oil and cultivated roses in the Imperial Gardens in Peking. Only the most distinguished persons were allowed to use the oil; ordinary mortals could at the most carry a few dried rose petals in a pouch as an amulet against evil spirits.

In China rose growing was regarded as a noble pursuit, but this land, closed to travellers, was reluctant to reveal its treasures. It was not until 1789 that three highly bred roses appeared – the result of at least three thousand years of breeding and selection – but of this, more later.

ROME – A TRUE ROSE GARDEN
The rose had already reached Rome before the birth of Christ. Pliny the Elder (23–79 A.D.) writes at length about it and names both wild species and cultivated forms with single and double flowers.

Although he mentions a rose with a hundred petals, this can no more be identified with *R.*

centifolia than that of Theophrastus. In Rome this was probably *R. gallica*, but it is just possible that it may have been *R. moschata* or *R. sempervirens*.

Here at the turning point of the ancient world, in splendour-loving Rome, the rose came to play an important role. The Romans loved the rose above all other flowers. It was used as a decoration for feasts and it adorned the chariots of returning victorious generals. Like everything else, it degenerated to an extravagance culminating in Nero (37–68 A.D.) having rose blooms rain down in his state dining room, so that some of the guests, so it is said, suffocated beneath the enormous mass of flowers.

The Romans also forced roses in beds under glass. They managed to obtain flowers long before nature intended. Winter roses – *hibernae rosae* – were praised as triumphs of horticulture; this rendered it unnecessary to import roses from Egypt, where according to Theophrastus the flowers appeared two months before those in Rome.

SUB ROSA

The Romans used enormous numbers of roses. Apart from decorating feasts and graves, the women used to put rose petals in their bath water. These were supposed to keep the body young and alluring – and at night, they put rose petals on their faces to keep away wrinkles.

The expression *sub rosa* also comes from this period; it means "beneath the rose" and derives from the ancient habit of hanging a rose above the guests at banquets, as a sign of the duty of maintaining discretion. This symbol is also found in many churches, where roses were hung above the confessional – an example of this can be seen in Worms Cathedral. The symbol of discretion is also to be found in old council chambers, as for example in Lübeck, where a rose is painted on the ceiling.

The Romans also knew about budding, that is the art of grafting a selected bud on to a wild rose.

In the later years of the Roman Empire the rose was linked more strongly with Venus, the goddess of love, and in the final phases of the

Fragment of a Roman tombstone from about 79 A.D. The robust candlestick is entwined by a delicate rose shoot; a couple of birds guard a little pile of lemons at the top.

Empire came to stand as a symbol of vice and non-chastity.

The period of Roman splendour was long since past, and the decay spread; the improved cultivated roses were no longer tended by skilled hands; houses fell into decay and gardens which had previously been so well cared for were left to run wild. Only the most robust varieties, with the necessary vigour for growth and propagation were able to survive in such conditions.

THE BLOOM OF APHRODITE BECOMES THE VIRGIN MARY'S FLOWER

After the fall of the Empire, the spiritual power of the Papacy was in the ascendancy. The Roman Catholic Church condemned the rose as a heathen flower and it was several centuries before this viewpoint changed.

The old church writers particularly condemned the heathen custom of offering wreaths of flowers to the dead: "If they are blessed, they do not need them – and if they are lost they won't have any pleasure in them". The custom, however, persisted and it became apparent that it would be necessary to associate the symbol, which was pagan in origin, with the culture of the Christian Church. The blood-red rose became a symbol of Jesus' blood.

The rose was then taken back into favour and even recognised as the sign of chastity. Aphrodite's flower became the flower of the Virgin Mary. One of the oldest Maria hymns says:

> *"Fresh rose, pure rose, chaste rose,*
> *Without thorns, rose flowering,*
> *Fruits bearing, burning red,*
> *More than a rose, whiter than the lily."*

Roses have often been found in the sarcophagi of the saints – indicating that the flower came to be regarded as an emblem of sanctity.

In 1049, Pope Leo IX instituted *The Order of the Golden Rose* which was originally conferred by the Pope's envoys on virtuous women. Later in the same century, *The Golden Rose* was bestowed on the church's great men and soon also on princes and ecclesiastical institutions. Thus for example

Christian I of Denmark was a recipient of the honour in 1474.

THE CHURCH'S ROSE WREATH

Later on, the Church opened wide its doors to the rose – and the rosary prayers were introduced. The prayers may possibly be regarded as a chaplet of roses dedicated to God, in any case we know that there were so-called "ritual" chaplets made of roses. Their form can be traced back to the Orient; in both India and Tibet for thousands of years, men have recited large numbers of prayers in order to attract the attention of the deity. Early on, this led to people using a string of beads, so that those praying could ascertain how much effort they had devoted to praying by letting a bead slip through their fingers for each prayer. At the time of the Crusades, it is known that both the Mohammedans and the Christians said their prayers in this way.

Even the rosary itself was sanctioned by the Pope in 1478. To ensure that one could be certain to say the correct number of prayers, the rosary was provided with large beads for Pater Nosters and smaller ones for Ave Marias.

In France during the thirteenth century, the use of garlands was so extensive that a special guild was established – *Les chapeliers de fleurs* – with permission to work on Sundays during the time that the roses were flowering.

The rose was regarded as a message from heaven to the earth's children, and it was considered that it would bring blessings if churches were built where roses grew. According to tradition the cathedral in Hildesheim was built alongside a wild rose, which still grows at the foot of the church.

In the rose windows of Gothic churches and in the colourful stained-glass windows, we also find evidence of the close connection between church and flower; the most beautiful examples of these are found in the cathedrals at Rheims, Chartres, Amiens, and also in Lincoln Cathedral and York Minster.

A connection is also found in the church feasts and in the churches' finger-bowls – in which rose

Madonna in the rose garden by Stephen Lochner (ca. 1410–1451). A meditation picture showing the use of the rose as a symbol of the Virgin Mary. We see the Virgin surrounded by roses — and she herself as a heavenly rose. The rose garden in the background is a symbol of paradise, a symbol that, like Christ as a gardener, is often seen in pictures of this period. This is one of the most famous Madonna paintings from the Renaissance, but many of the other fifteenth- and sixteenth-century masters used the same motif of the Virgin Mary surrounded by roses. Comparison of these pictures shows that the predominant roses of the period were R. gallica and varieties of R. alba.

The rosary was often used as a motif in the decoration of churches; here is the centre part of the Late Gothic altarpiece in Hviding Church, Denmark. The relief is encircled by fifty small roses for Ave Marias, interspersed at regular intervals by five large roses for the Lord's Prayer.

water was used. In Salency, for example, the clerics instituted an annual rose feast which is still carried on today.

THE MIDDLE AGES

The earliest historical sources on the new medieval folk culture of Europe mention very little about roses.

The first European rose garden that is known is the one King Childebert (died 558), who lived in Paris, laid out for his wife.

Manuscripts show that rose growing came to the western parts of Germany in about 800 A.D. Charlemagne (or perhaps his son) ordered that roses be planted in the castles in the Palatinate.

During the age of chivalry and troubadours, the rose came to play a more worldly role. The rose was the symbol of love, a symbol to which the minnesingers in particular paid great atten-

tion – in their courtly verses to the praise of women.

At the same time, these epics of heroes and of common people describe the medieval rose gardens, where a varied worldly and religious life unfolded itself behind the tall thorny bushes and scented espaliers.

It was the monks who introduced gardening into North Europe. In 1165, Abbot William, was called to Denmark by Bishop Absalom where he established his monastery garden on Eskilsø, but one can only guess whether he had roses in this garden.

This however was the route by which grafts and seeds came to Denmark and we can reckon that cultivated roses from southern Europe had reached Scandinavia, the Low Countries, northern France and England by the second half of the twelfth century.

The Holy Roman Emperor Sigismund (1411–37) with the Golden Rose order which the Pope had conferred on him in Constance.

The first mention of roses in Danish literature is in Henrik Harpestreng's Herbal which dates from the first half of the thirteenth century, and as they are called *rosae*, it is natural to assume that they had already been grown for some time.

During the following centuries, roses became widespread. The Crusaders brought home new and old varieties, and it seems that it was by this method that the Damask Rose arrived in Europe in 1270 for the second time from the Holy Land.

It was natural enough that the rose should become particularly popular in France. We can be sure that roses became the favourite adornment for the table and for personal attire. The flower was also used in medicine, and its cultivation steadily increased. The town of Rouen, well

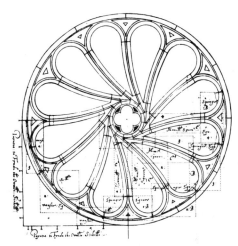

An English architectural drawing of 1599, with specifications for the construction of a rose-window.

known for its Gothic cathedral, became the centre for rose-growing.

THE ROSE AS A MEDICINAL HERB

As a medicinal herb, the rose has its own history; mention has already been made of the fact that Roman ladies knew about the rejuvenating power of rose petals, about how to transfer the scent of roses to olive oil and how to prepare rose water. It was not until about 300 years ago, however – around the middle of the seventeenth century – that man succeeded in making pure attar of roses.

Nowadays, this product is made particularly in Bulgaria (Tundzha and Kasanlik – in the district known as "Rose Valley") and in France, but the amount produced is not large; it takes about 3 million rose flowers or 10,000 lbs of rose petals to make 1 lb of attar.

In the late Middle Ages, the oil was used in the treatment of eye complaints – a little rose oil smeared around weak and swollen eyes was said to remove all pain.

In addition to rose oil and rose water, the medieval apothecaries also prepared rose honey, rose vinegar and rose conserve. The latter was made by pounding fresh rose petals with sugar or honey in a mortar, and the result was a much sought-after gift among princes and rich men.

Two beautiful and typical circular windows based on the rose, in the west face of Rheims Cathedral; end of thirteenth century.

The Roman de la Rose *was one of the earliest poems in which the rose played a part. The first part of this allegorical poem was written about 1220 by Guillaume de Lorris, the latter half about 1270 by Jean de Meung. The poem describes a dream in which the poet in his travels comes to a beautiful garden, Love's Paradise. Here he meets various allegorical persons, but forgets everything at the sight of a rosebud, which becomes a symbol of his beloved. He has to go through severe trials but finally reaches his rose with the help of Venus herself. This picture, from an edition about one hundred years later, shows the poet's meeting with the rose.*

The conserves, moreover, were prescribed for lung and liver complaints. Rose vinegar was used for several purposes – the alleviation of nose bleeding, headache, an upset stomach and so on. Rose sugar was said to be effective against consumption.

One of the old medical books gives recipes for many of these remedies. The recipes differentiated between the effects, which were supposed to be dependent upon the colour of the rose – but they added that it was best to allow the apothecary to give advice "as he had been properly trained in this art".

Rose water can still be bought at a pharmacist's, and is still used as an eyebath; it is also a constituent of many recipes for face lotions – so what the Roman ladies discovered 2000 years ago is still valid today.

An old tradition also talks about the rose – Aphrodite's flower – as a love potion. A girl should wear a red, a white and a pink rose on her breast for three days and then put the roses into wine for a further three days. If she gives her chosen one this wine to drink, he becomes hers.

Nowadays, however, it is the fruits or hips which are particularly valued, on account of their high content of vitamin C; jam is mostly made from the Japanese Rose, *R. rugosa*.

THE RED AND THE YELLOW ROSE

In a legend from the tenth century a German scribe tells that the Creator had roses and white lilies planted in Paradise. The rose was just as white as the lily, but it suddenly changed its colour out of shame for Eve's disobedience and became the red rose, whilst the lily remained white.

One story seems to have given the yellow rose

Illustration from Champier's Rosa Gallica *(Paris 1515). The learned doctor is lecturing on the virtues and characteristics of the rose.*

Headpiece to the ballad on the rose garden in the German Heldenbuch (ca. 1500).

ROSES IN THE MIDDLE AGES

At this period of history, the roses in cultivation were the Provence or French rose (*R. gallica plena*), the white rose (*R. x alba*) and the introduced *R. damascena* and hybrids between them. The Cabbage Rose, (*R. centifolia*) was sterile and could not therefore contribute to further improvement. The rose most commonly grown in monastery gardens around the 1400s was the Provence rose.

The Romans differentiated between a rose nursery, or *rosetum*, and a rose garden, or *rosarium*. In the twelfth century roses were planted in hedges and tied to sticks, espaliers and lattices. Paintings show the Madonna in front of a wall of roses and rose arbours often appear in old drawings. The true rose gardens, from which the art of breeding roses developed, did not however appear until the late Middle Ages.

In *The Decameron*, Boccaccio (1313–1375) describes gardens with red and white roses in flower beds.

THE WARS OF THE ROSES

In 1455, the Houses of York and Lancaster were contending for the throne of England. The supporters of York wore a white rose which is still known today; it is *R. alba incarnata*, a form with

an everlasting title of falsehood. This took place in 612 A.D. when Mohammed was fighting the Jews. While he was away, his favourite wife, Ayesha, bestowed her favours on a young Persian. When Mohammed came home to Medina, he was tormented by uncertainty about Ayesha's faithfulness, and so he sent for advice to the angel Gabriel. Gabriel appeared to him in a dream and said: "Ask her to dip some object into the palace well. If she is innocent, the object will remain unchanged, if she is guilty, its colour will change." The next day, Mohammed asked Ayesha, who was sitting by the palace well with a pretty spray of roses, to dip it in the water, which she did, laughing loudly. When she pulled it out, it was brilliant saffron-yellow.

Illustration from the German Heldenbuch (c. 1500). The Knights Dietlieb von Steir and Walther von Wachsenstein, returning from a successful combat, receive garlands of roses for their services.

double white flowers and a pale delicate pink tinge. The red rose of Lancaster is thought to have been *R. gallica* "Red Damask", although this is not certain.

When the war ended, it is said that a gardener named Miellez contributed to the reconciliation by crossing the white and the red rose, thus creating the red-and-white striped Tudor rose.

From the end of the Middle Ages until the period before the French Revolution attempts were made to improve the cultivated rose by hybridising it with *R. eglanteria, R. cinnamonea, R. spinosissima* and others, but these lacked the hereditary characteristics present in the roses which the Chinese guarded so strenuously behind the high mountains of Asia.

THE RENAISSANCE

During the sixteenth century it was the fashion for princes, noblemen and rich merchants to collect roses. *Rosaria* became more interesting as collections of rarities than as ornamental gardens. This interest in collecting resulted in the spread of species and hybrids; the study of botany grew at this time, doubtless encouraged by the amount of material made available through the interest in collecting.

Roses appear in the Renaissance paintings of Raphael, Michaelangelo and Leonardo da Vinci, and in Florence Sandro Botticelli painted his charming versions. In Holland Jan Brueghel the Elder – often called "Velvet Brueghel" – lived from 1525 to 1569, and in his paintings we can see many of the species and varieties already mentioned.

NEW ROSES – NEW POSSIBILITIES

New roses were introduced at regular intervals – one called "Rosa majalis" was *R. cinnamonea plena*. The "Holy Franciscus Rose" has been

Rosa lutea

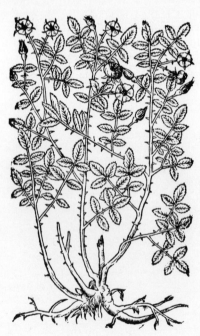

Rosa eglanteria

Woodcuts from Neu vollkommen Kräuterbuch, *1687, by D. Jacobus Theodorus Tabernaemontanus.*

Work in a rose grove. Tying up rose shoots around a bench. A romantic setting for two lovers. After an engraving of ca. 1600.

shown to be *R. centifolia parviflora* – that is, a true centifolia rose. Around 1580, the yellow rose, *R. lutea*, was introduced from Asia Minor; nowadays its varieties are included in *R. x foetida*.

Two old varieties from the Renaissance period, which are still in cultivation, are the Capuchin

The Tudor Rose, which after the Wars of the Roses (1455–85) symbolised the reconciliation between the houses of York and Lancaster, is often found on articles associated with King Henry VII (1485–1509). Just as the rose was used in the coinage of Rhodes (see p. 11) so it was also used on this coin from King Henry's reign.

Persian Yellow.

The musk rose, *R. moschata*, which is a tall-growing, climbing species with a slight scent of musk was introduced from the Himalayas and later became a valuable parent species.

At the end of the sixteenth century and the beginning of the seventeenth the focal point for the production of new roses moved to Holland. Dutch gardeners set to work on the centifolia roses and developed a large number of varieties. Here, mutations, that is sudden changes in the hereditary make-up, produced the moss rose, *R. centifolia muscosa*, in which the glands on the sepals and leaf stalks are developed into curly green scales giving a moss-like appearance. The Dutch, who had had "tulipomania", found a new pursuit and over 2000 varieties of centifolia and moss roses arose.

UNSUITABLE FOR GARDEN CULTIVATION

With the Baroque period in the seventeenth and eighteenth centuries the cultivation of roses received a significant setback. One could not allow untidy rose beds to protrude among the formal beds, neatly edged with box. Later when it became fashionable to have natural gardens –

the advent of the English style of free landscape-gardening – roses again moved into the gardens as bushes or as ramblers for arbours and fences.

Although there were many beautiful varieties, the roses of that period had two big drawbacks as garden plants: growth was untidy and the leaves were not particularly decorative, so they were

The rose garden is the motif in this romantic miniature of an Elizabethan nobleman painted by Nicholas Hilliard (1537–1619). This use of the rose is typical of the period. On her coat of arms Queen Elizabeth herself had the motto, "a rose without a thorn".

best suited for training against a wall or tied back to hang down over a balustrade.

However, their greatest failing was that they only flowered once a year. It is true that they flowered profusely but for the rest of the summer the bushes were bare.

At the end of the eighteenth century, when links were forged with the distant colonies, many new genera of flowering plants arrived, such as the dahlia, the narcissus, peonies, and all these became very popular.

Cabbage and Damask roses could still trace their ancestry back to Persia; but the long association with man had set them in a definite form; it had produced as much variation as the hereditary material would allow, for there was a natural limit – the chromosome barrier. Much was lacking in the beauty of the petals, in the form of the flower and in particular the period of flowering was very restricted. Development had stopped – the rose had reached a period of crisis.

NEW INCENTIVES

Life in France was in a state of ferment. Thinking was now centred on the liberty of the people, on freeing them from the yoke of the monarchy. These ideas were germinating and influencing the peoples' lives and their politics and philosophy.

Although one cannot really point to a connection, it was at this time that new genes were introduced to the roses of France from the Far East, from China and India. The first rose from eastern Asia arrived in 1768; this was the China Rose, *R. chinensis*, a harbinger of rich promise. This rose probably came originally from northern Burma and was possibly introduced into Chinese gardens about the year 600. For centuries, Chinese gardeners had grappled with this delicate rose, and had succeeded in making it hardy and long-flowering. Then it was brought from Canton to Europe.

The big breakthrough took place, in fact, at the same time as the French Revolution, for the dark-red, perpetually flowering form of the China Rose, *R. chinensis semperflorens*, was introduced in 1789. It is thought that these were really three very different species, all of which however flowered throughout the summer. Unfortunately, loss of scent went with this step forward, and these species passed on this lack of scent to their progeny.

In the year 1800, there was no one who knew about genetics or had heard of chromosomes. Gardeners and plant lovers used the "natural method" and brought pollen from the new Chinese species to the old.

What now happened had something to do with the chromosomes which carry the hereditary material or genes. The roses from the East have only 14 chromosomes in their cell nuclei, whereas the western species have 28. When a European female flower with 28 chromosomes was pollinated by a Chinese male flower, the result was a series of very vigorous roses with 21 chromosomes. This is all explained in more detail in the section entitled "How a new rose is created" (page 53). This development has certainly shown us that fantasy and intuition can often bring about remarkable results.

THE ROSE GARDEN AT MALMAISON

At this period, an important event in the history of the rose took place. Revolution is succeeded by evolution. Napoleon came to power after the French Revolution and his wife Josephine became Empress in 1804; the garden which she established at Malmaison, six miles west of Paris, became the focal point of a new interest in roses.

Josephine instructed a skilled gardener, Dupont, to lay out a rose garden with all the best varieties that could be found; she herself arranged for them to be sent home through diplomatic channels from all over Europe. She collected all the most beautiful roses she could and when in 1809 she ceased to be Napoleon's wife, Malmaison became her retreat. She lived there among her roses until 1814.

She was visited in this palace by Tsar Alexander I of Russia who had undertaken to console her and to convey an assurance of support from the allied princely houses. The Empress awaited him in her salon which her head gardener, Bonpland, had decorated with the year's first roses. Alexander

Characteristic use of roses on a title page of 1644. Besides being very decorative the rose shoots also emphasise the nature of the book's love story.

saw immediately that he had come too late; both were much moved and words failed them; Josephine took one of the roses out of the vase and handed it to the Tsar – whose chivalry much affected her – a Souvenir de la Malmaison.

These words were later used to name a delicate pink rose which was raised in 1845 by Beluze, a nurseryman in Lyons.

LES ROSES

The great baroque artist Rubens was a passionate lover of roses and he used its heavy blooms to frame his exuberant characters, in such a way

The Empress Josephine, wife of Napoleon, whose work with roses has been of unique value in later times. In the garden of Malmaison outside Paris she instructed her gardener, Dupont, to lay out a beautiful rose garden, for which she obtained all the roses known at the time. There they were cultivated and much important work on propagation was carried out (engraved from the painting by Prud'hon. Louvre).

that both figures and flowers form part of the composition. In the period which followed, the Dutch painters became absorbed in representing all the intimate details of the flower, as though they were making a botanical drawing. They created a series of beautiful flower pictures, but finally developed a cult of exaggerated naturalism, in which the minute rendering of detail destroyed all life and feeling.

The period after Josephine saw a noble array of garden roses, and, developing from the exaggerated naturalism of the Dutch painters,

there came a masterpiece. In conjunction with C. A. Thory, the artist, Pierre-Joseph Redouté (1759–1840), published an illustrated book, *Les Roses*, during the period 1817–1820, which had 160 colour plates. This book had the best of the Dutch naturalism combined with Gallic elegance. It was illustrative art of the highest quality.

Redouté himself came from a family of painters, and at the age of fifteen made his own way through the Low Countries, studying the works of the old masters. Eight years later he settled finally in Paris and to begin with spent a great deal of time drawing plants in the Jardins du Roi. A well-known botanist, C. L. L'Héritier de Brutelle, helped him and eventually took him to England where Pierre-Joseph met Bartolozzi, the engraver. Back in France he became assistant to Gérard van Spaëndonck (whose flower engravings rank among the finest ever done), and then was court-artist just before the Revolution. Eventually he was commissioned by Josephine to draw the flowers at Malmaison. The first folio of *Les Roses* contained 170 plates; the first octavo edition had 160 and the second about 180.

Redouté's book is still reprinted today with the original plates, and the contemporary pictures he gives of the roses of his period are unique. They are principally the forms that gave rise to our modern varieties, but the collection also contains the first two hybrids, the Noisette Rose and the Bourbon Rose.

The Noisette Rose first appeared in America in 1802 from where it reached the Malmaison garden; it was a hybrid between the Musk Rose, *R. moschata*, and *R. chinensis*. The Bourbon Rose appeared in 1817 on the island of Bourbon (now Réunion) in the Indian Ocean.

FROM 200 TO 16,000 VARIETIES

There are several other Asiatic roses. The red-flowered *Rosa odorata* – probably a natural hybrid – came from China. It was the true tea rose of the Orient.

In England in 1838, a rose seedling flowered which eventually exerted a strong influence on future development. It was the first tea rose to be raised in Europe. Called Devoniensis (coming from Devon) it became the true ancestor of our later, much-beloved tea roses and their hybrids. It was not very hardy but the fine petals gave grace, lightness and scent to the roses of today.

Progress was rather slow in the early stages; at the beginning of the eighteenth century, there were 200–400 varieties and species. From 1823 to 1843 only 43 new roses were produced, but by 1850 the total was over 1000. In the last edition of Jager's *Rosenlexicon* (Uftringer, 1936) some 16,000 varieties were listed on 768 pages.

ROSES AND THEIR NAMES

We now come to the pleasant custom of naming roses after people. The gardener naturally thinks first of himself and his family but his loyalties, sense of deference and honour or snobbery also play a part, and roses are named after members of royalty or influential people. To use a rose for self-advertisement is not a new idea. Thousands of people have allowed their name to be used. Many well-known people have had their names tied to less good roses, whilst unknown persons have become known through roses which received world renown.

The breeders of roses have become known far beyond the boundaries of their own country. Who has not heard of the roses produced by the Poulsen family? From the early days of rose rearing, we have names such as Vibert (France), Plantier (France), Guillot (France), Ducher (France), Pernet (France), Lambert (Germany), Spath (Germany), Dickson (Northern Ireland), Perkins (U.S.A.), and more recently Kordes (Germany), Tantau (Germany), Mallerin (France), Armstrong (U.S.A.), McGredy (Northern Ireland), Le Grice (England), Robinson (England), Meilland (France), Dot (Spain) and Gaujard (France).

In the early nineteenth century, roses were mostly named after the gentry. In Jager's *Rosenlexicon* there are pages of varieties named Madame ... and later Mrs ... In 1846, a Frenchman, Bélot-Defougère, respecting his lady's anonymity, called his rose "Souvenir d'un ami". Other

Pierre-Joseph Redouté (1759–1840), the creator of the beautiful and immortal work – Les Roses.

nineteenth-century rose names were long ones, such as Souvenir de Madame Salati-Mongellaz, Archiduchesse Marie Immaculate or Beauty of Waltham.

GODDESSES, PRINCESSES AND GENERALS

About the turn of the century roses were often named after goddesses or muses: Hebe, Euphrosyne, Aglaia, Euterpe, Terpsichore, Thalia, Nivea and Urania. Others were called after characters in poetry, opera and music, and we find Ophelia, Lady Godiva, Carmen, Madame Butterfly, La Tosca and many others.

The deference of gardeners is reflected in such long names as Baronne Nathaniel de Rothschild, Docteur Andry, Geheimrat Duisberg, Gartendirektor Glocker, Grace de Monaco, or more recently Parkdirektor Riggers.

Patriotism has occasionally found expression in rose names, and here La France occupies a special place. This was reared in Lyons in 1867 by the well-known nurseryman firm of M. Guillot Fils. This was a particularly fine rose, elegant and well-scented, of a pale peach colour, a silvery pink. It was a delicate expression of French feeling and it became the rose of the century.

Military men have often had their names preserved – sometimes for longer than their own renown. For instance, a hundred years after a rose was given the name Maréchal Niel, few people remember, even in France, that he led an army corps at the Battle of Solferino and in 1867 became the Minister of War who saw to it that French soldiers got breech-loading rifles. But the rose is still known, even though there is scant connection between the name and this delicate flower – described by the Germans as a "dreamy rose".

In England a rose was named K. of K. in 1917 – an abbreviation for Lord Kitchener of Khartoum.

A WEALTH OF POSSIBILITIES

In England, the giving of names continued on the basis of drawing comparisons with beauty, as for example: Sunstar, Gardenia, Rubin, Silver Moon and more recently Coral Dawn, Golden Showers, Crimson Glory, Geranium, Starlet and Shepherd's Delight.

In Germany, it became common to name roses after towns and cities, to such an extent that one breeder acquired a sort of monopoly. The big German firm of Kordes, the creator of numerous roses, used such names as the following for a certain type of perpetual flowering bush rose: Berlin, Bonn, Hamburg, Mannheim, Saarbrucken, Sparrieshoop. This is a particularly practical method; it corresponds to the naming of streets from a given class – e.g. flowers, literary men, etc. and it provides many possibilities. This successful method was continued with another bush rose, for which the prefix Frühling (spring) was used: Frühlingsanfang, -duft, -gold, -morgen, -schnee and Frühlingszauber.

In recent years, dances have provided the motif, particularly among the floribunda varieties: Polka, Dans de Feu, Flammentanz, Polonaise, Rumba, Farandole, Toni Lander, Ballet and Prima Ballerina.

Nowadays short, sonorous names have become popular because they quickly capture the public's attention. The great rose breeder Francis Meilland has achieved this in such names as Radar, Alain, Cocorico, Exita, Marella, Zambra, Baccara, Caprice and Sarabande.

CONFUSION OF NAMES

It is unfortunate when the same rose receives different names. This may be done to hide the original name. At the First International Horticultural Exhibition, held at Chelsea in 1913, the *Daily Mail* offered a prize of £1000 for the most beautiful rose in the show. An English nurseryman had obtained a French rose called Madame Edouard Herriot, named after the wife of the Mayor of Lyons, which he forced in pots. This rose won the prize, but the newspaper made a condition that the rose should be called Daily Mail. The original breeder Pernet refused to re-christen his rose. He preferred to lose money rather than hurt the feelings of his friend Herriot who later became Prime Minister. So for many years the rose was called Madame Edouard Herriot in France and Daily Mail in England.

It was more a matter of politics which affected the French rose, Madame A. Meilland, produced in 1942. With due festivity this was introduced to the United States in 1945, the year of peace, as Peace. This masterpiece from the famous rose breeder of Antibes is called Gloria Dei in Germany and Gioia in Italy. It is to be hoped that this unsatisfactory procedure will not become widespread.

THE ROSE IN ENGLISH LITERATURE

Throughout the ages the rose has captured the imagination of poets. Nearly all our writers have extolled its virtues, associating it with beauty, fragrance, romantic and mystical love. Many of the best references are linked with the loveliness

Rosa centifolia Bullata.

Rosier à feuilles de Laitue.

P. J. Redouté pinx.

Imprimerie de Rémond

Langlois sculp

One of the illustrations from Redouté's Les Roses, *which was published in France in the period
1817–20.*

of woman and the transience of youth and beauty.

The allegory attributed to Chaucer, "The Romaunt of the Rose", translated from a French poem already a century old, is an early example of the tradition of rose-symbolism already well established in mediaeval times. It tells of the poet's dream of his beloved, Rosebud, in the Garden of Love, and his final winning of her after many difficulties.

Shakespeare made many references to the rose, both in his dramas and his sonnets. He seems to have been well acquainted with the different species known in his time and pays tribute, in particular, to the musk rose (*R. moschata*), the white rose of York (*R. alba*), the red rose of Lancaster (*R. gallica*), the rose of Provence, and their hybrids. He loved the fragrant roses, the Sweet Briar (*R. eglanteria*) being a particular favourite because of its scented leaves. It was *R. moschata* and *R. eglanteria* which adorned Titania's bower (A Midsummer Night's Dream, Act 2, Scene 1):

"I know a bank whereon the wild thyme blows,
Where oxlips and the nodding violet grows,
Quite o'er-canopied with lush woodbine,
With sweet musk roses and with eglantine;
There sleeps Titania sometime of the night
Lulled in these flowers with dances and delight."

The resentment of the young lovers, Romeo and Juliet, to the quarrel between the Houses of the Montagues and the Capulets is expressed by Juliet who, after suggesting to Romeo that he should deny his father and refuse to be a Montague, says, that if he will not, she will no longer be a Capulet. "After all," she says:

"What's Montague? it is nor hand nor foot
Nor arm, nor face, nor any other part
Belonging to a man. O be some other name!
What's in a name? that which we call a rose
By any other name would smell as sweet!"

In "Twelfth Night", Act 2, Scene 4, Shakespeare makes striking use of the rose-image when Viola says of Olivia in reply to the Duke's suit of that lady's hand:

". . . She never told her love,
But let concealment, like a worm i' the bud,
Feed on her damask cheek."

Shakespeare also makes several references to the white rose of York and the red rose of Lancaster, notably in "Henry VI, Part I", Act 2, Scene 4, the quarrel in the garden of the Inner Temple which is said to have led to the Wars of the Roses. This scene has a typically Elizabethan elaboration on the theme of roses. Even today the county feeling in England for the white and red roses of Yorkshire and Lancashire is still very strong:

"RICHARD PLANTAGENET:
Since you are tongue-tied and so loth to speak,
In dumb significants proclaim your thoughts:
Let him that is a true-born gentleman,
And stands upon the honour of his birth,
If he suppose that I have pleaded truth,
From off this briar pluck a white rose with me.

EARL OF SOMERSET:
Let him that is no coward, nor no flatterer,
But dare maintain the party of the truth,
Pluck a red rose from off this thorn with me.

EARL OF WARWICK:
I love no colours: and, without all colour
Of base insinuating flattery
I pluck this white rose with Plantagenet.

EARL OF SUFFOLK:
I pluck this red rose with young Somerset,
And say withal I think he held the right.

VERNON:
Stay, lords and gentlemen, and pluck no more,
Till you conclude that he, upon whose side
The fewest roses from the tree are cropp'd
Shall yield the other in the right opinion.

EARL OF SOMERSET:
Good Master Vernon, it is well objected;
If I have fewest, I subscribe in silence.

RICHARD PLANTAGENET:
And I.

VERNON:

Then for the truth and plainness of the case,
I pluck this pale and maiden blossom here,
Giving my verdict on the white rose side.

EARL OF SOMERSET:

Prick not your finger as you pluck it off,
Lest, bleeding, you do paint the white rose red,
And fall on my side so against your will.

VERNON:

If I, my lord, for my opinion bleed,
Opinion shall be surgeon to my hurt
And keep me on the side where still I am."

The poetic rose is the perfect flower, but not all the roses of Shakespeare's day were memorable for their fragrance, as Francis Bacon, who observed the natural world with a different kind of eye, points out in his "Essay on Gardens":

"Roses, damask and red are fast flowers of their smells;
so that you may walk by a whole row of them and find
nothing of their sweetness; yea, though it be in a
morning's dew."

The poets of the 16th and 17th centuries are continually invoking the rose to suggest the fleeting nature of youth and beauty. Edmund Spenser's lines in Book 2, Canto 12, of the "Faerie Queene":

"Gather therefore the Rose, whilst yet is prime,
For soon comes age, that will her pride deflower;
Gather the rose of love, whilst yet is time,
Whilst loving thou mayst loved be with equal crime."

find an echo in the "Wooing Song" of Giles Fletcher (the younger):

"Every thing doth pass away,
There is danger in delay,
Come, come, gather then the rose,
Gather it, or it ye lose!"

and in Robert Herrick's famous advice to the Virgins to make the most of their youth:

"Gather ye rosebuds while ye may,
Old Time is still a-flying:

And this same flower that smiles today
Tomorrow will be dying."

The same thought is found in Edmund Waller's magnificent lyric "Go, Lovely Rose":

"Go, lovely Rose!
Tell her that wastes her time and me
That now she knows
When I resemble her to thee
How sweet and fair she seems to be."

In the masque, John Milton puts these words about Beauty into the mouth of Comus:

"If you let slip Time, like a neglected rose
It withers on the stalk with languished head."

But to the 19th-century American poet William Cullen Bryant it is precisely this quality that gives to the rose its special charm:

"Loveliest of lovely things are they
On earth that soonest pass away,
The rose that lives its little hour
Is prized beyond the sculptured flower."

From an engraving by William Blake.

From the rose as a stock-in-trade image of sophisticated or pastoral verse it is a far cry to "The Sick Rose" of William Blake, a poem that in its vivid and disturbing evocation of destructive love has a force far beyond the literal meaning of the words:

> "O Rose, thou art sick.
> The invisible worm,
> That flies in the night
> In the howling storm:
>
> Has found out thy bed
> Of crimson joy:
> And his dark secret love
> Does thy life destroy."

In the poetry of the late 18th and early 19th centuries the rose is as prolific as before. It crops up in Wordsworth, Coleridge, Byron, Shelley and Keats, as well as in a host of minor figures of the time; and of course in the lyric of Robert Burns it has one of its best-known settings:

> "O my Luve's like a red, red rose
> That's newly sprung in June:
> O my Luve's like the melodie
> That's sweetly play'd in tune!"

Shelley has the memorable lines:

> "Rose leaves, when the rose is dead
> Are heaped for my beloved's bed;
> And so thy thoughts, when thou art gone,
> Love itself shall slumber on."

Keats extols the fragrance of the musk rose he so dearly loved in his sonnet "To a friend who sent me some roses", and Wordsworth too, in his "Intimations of Immortality" Ode, finds the rose beautiful for its own sake:

> "The rainbow comes and goes,
> And lovely is the rose;"

Later in the 19th century there are references to the rose in, among others, Robert Browning ("Women and Roses"), in Tennyson many times, in Matthew Arnold, in Elizabeth Barrett Browning, whose "A Lay of the Early Rose" suggests a sound knowledge of varieties:

> " 'For if I wait,' said she,
> 'Till time for roses be,
> For the moss-rose and the musk-rose,
> Maiden-Blush and royal-dusk rose,
> What glory then for me
> In such a company?
> Roses plenty, roses plenty,
> And one nightingale for twenty!' "

In fairyland everything is possible. This drawing from Lewis Carroll's Through the Looking Glass *shows Alice talking to flowers in the garden. She is busy conversing seriously with the roses, who are insinuating that she is unable to think.*

in George Eliot's "Spanish Gypsy", Book 3, a thought that will give the practical gardener a great deal of satisfaction:

> "It never will rain roses: when we want
> To have more roses we must plant more trees."

in Edward Fitzgerald's translation of "The Rubáiyát" of Omar Khayyám, and in Ernest Dowson's famous poem "Non Sum Qualis Eram Bonae sub Regno Cynarae":

"I have forgot much, Cynara, gone with the wind,
Flung roses, roses, riotously with the throng,
Dancing, to put thy pale lost lilies out of mind."

In modern times the rose has continued to appeal to the poetic imagination. The early poetry of W. B. Yeats and the opening of T. S. Eliot's "Burnt Norton" show that in spite of centuries of hard use it is still a symbol of great power; here, finally, is a section from the beginning of "Burnt Norton":

"Footfalls echo in the memory
Down the passage which we did not take
Towards the door we never opened
Into the rose-garden. My words echo
Thus, in your mind.
                        But to what purpose
Disturbing the dust on a bowl of rose-leaves
I do not know."

"... the roses from the eaves grew in at the open window ...
and Kay and Gerda looked into one another's eyes and immed-
iately understood the old hymn
   The roses grow in the valleys
   Where we shall talk to the infant Jesus."
An illustration by Vilhelm Pedersen in Hans Andersen's Snow
Queen. This great writer has also used the rose motif in various
other stories, for example, The loveliest rose in the world,
The snail and the rose hedge, Rose fairy, Little Ida's
flowers.

SCENT OF ROSES

Since the rose ranks so high among plants, it is natural that its characteristics should be used and misused in the service of advertisement. Advertisements for property link the flower with many towns such as Roseville. Restaurants or parts of them are often called Rosecourt or Rose Garden or Rose Lounge and here one finds that the rose motif is used in the interior decoration.

The perfume industry, with its centre at Grasse in the neighbourhood of Cannes, fully exploits the popularity of the rose. The health concept often makes use of the association of roses, as, for example, "rose skin", while advertisers have made a point of linking scent and beautiful women in the pictures they put on packets of scent and soap.

The well known rose Mme Caroline Testout provides a good example of how a rose name can advertise a person. This rose was produced in Lyons in 1891 (as an improvement of the rose, La France) and a dressmaker managed to get her name affixed to it. She could scarcely expect immortality in her own trade, nevertheless her name lives in this rose in the gardens of the world. It became so popular in England that it was called the Slave of the Rose Garden.

THE ROSE TODAY

The movement of roses from the East has now stopped. Roses are here and the East has become united with the West.

"What a lot of beauty you have given us", said a New York journalist to a rose breeder who had created several new varieties. "No", he replied as he sat on his campstool among the roses, transferring pollen from one variety to the stigma of another. "The Creator has given roses the inherent possibilities; it is our job to use these hereditary characters, and we enjoy doing so. I myself have not created anything, I have only been a manager and an administrator."

Every year new and beautiful roses are created – and every day roses are being used as a sign of friendship, of love, of joy and of expectation.

Roses from the Middle Ages still bloom in our

church windows, Renaissance and Baroque roses adorn Dutch and Italian paintings, and Josephine's roses stand out from the beautiful colour plates of Redouté. Old rose gardens still have Souvenir de la Malmaison, La France, Soleil d'Or, Cardinal's Hat and Red Letter Day.

Such old roses are preserved at two places in Europe. The Roseraie de l'Hay-les-Roses at Sceaux near Paris was started in 1893 by Jules Gravereaux, who set out to collect all Josephine's roses as well as those subsequently produced from them. Everything is well arranged and labelled and there is a museum for the treasures of the rose's history. There is also a very large collection at Sangerhausen in East Germany, but it is said to have suffered during and after the Second World War.

Nowadays every country and almost every town has its rose garden. These are the places where rose lovers forgather, and where the ordinary man's awareness of the riches of today is awakened. There are hybrid perpetual bushes and colourful displays of floribunda roses, the modern descendants of the polyantha roses; climbing roses deck the hedges, and the fine hybrid tea roses are once more increasing in popularity.

Woodcut from A. Lonicerus' Kreuterbuch, *1679.*

Key to the plate of hips on the opposite page: a. R. gallica, *b. Frühlingsmorgen, c.* R. spinosissima, *d.* R. pendula, *e.* R. rugosa *Dagmar Hastrup, f.* R. moyesii, *g.* R. virginiana *and* R. carolina, *h.* R. eglanteria, *i.* R. blanda, *j. Lucy Bertram, k.* R. multiflora, *l.* R. helenae.

At the end of the nineteenth century, excavation of King Minos' Palace at Knossos in Crete revealed the first pictures of ancient roses. It will be seen that the flowers have six petals instead of five, but the foliage is of the typical rose type.

In writing of the rose, Greek and Roman authors were referring to Rosa gallica and Rosa damascena. In early times, the rose was associated with Aphrodite, the goddess of love — the symbol of beauty, but also of frivolity and unchastity. Much later, however, the Roman Catholic Church raised the rose to a symbol of purity associated with the Virgin Mary.

Rosa gallica

Rosa damascena

Throughout the ages, the rose has had a prominent place in decoration. In former times a stylised rose pattern was used on the capitals of columns, and also in the form of rosettes.

The circular form of ornamentation is oriental in origin; it was used in several ways in the East. In Europe, it was frequently employed in the design of rose windows in churches.

Some fine examples of rose-windows in brilliantly coloured stained glass can be seen in the Cathedrals at Lincoln, Chartres and Rheims.

In 1455, civil war broke out between the rival houses of York and Lancaster. This became a bitter struggle which only ended with the death of Richard III at Bosworth. The conflict became known as the Wars of the Roses on account of the emblems carried by the

Rosa mundi

Rosa damascena

Rosa alba

Lancaster

York

two sides, York having a white and Lancaster a red rose. When the war ended and the house of Tudor came into power, the red-and-white rose produced by the English gardener Miellez became a symbol of reconciliation.

In the *Avesta*, the sacred book of Persia, which is held to form the basis of one of the world's oldest religions, the rose appears as a religious symbol. Remains of a rose cult have, in fact, been found in several parts of the Middle East. When the Arabs and Islam reached Persia they found that flowers were being extensively cultivated. From there the Moslem religion spread to large areas of the known world and with it went the rose.

The rose of Persia was yellow, like, for example, the Sulphur Rose (*Rosa sulphurea*) and *Rosa foetida*, and in many of our modern roses the yellow strain can be traced back to this ancient centre of culture. Persian artists often used the rose motif in their paintings, as for instance in this miniature of a young prince carrying a rose.

Rosa foetida

Rosa sulfurea

In Persia the rose motif was used not only in paintings, but also in textiles, tapestries and carpets. Here is a piece of seventeenth-century Persian brocade with a rose forming the centre of the design.

From 1809 to 1814, Napoleon's wife, the Empress Josephine, lived in the Malmaison not far from Paris, and there she created a rose garden that was unsurpassed. The new Asiatic roses had begun to arrive in Europe shortly before the turn of the century; these and many other roses from Europe and elsewhere were gathered together in this garden. Skilled gardeners tended and propagated these plants which constituted the largest collection hitherto seen. It was due to the pioneer work at Malmaison that a few years later (in 1817), it was possible to cross one of the new Asiatic varieties with an old Western rose. This was done on the French island of Bourbon in the Indian Ocean, which gave its name to the new rose — Rosa bourboniana.

Malmaison

Rosa bourboniana

Rosa indica

5

Alain

Allgold

Ama

6

Ballet

Baccara

7

Betty Prior

Belle Blonde

Bettina

Betty Uprichard

Buccaneer

9

Champs Elysées

Charles Bonnet

Chinatown

Christopher Stone

11

Circus

Columbine   Concerto

Chrysler
Imperial

Cynthia Brooke

13

Cricri

Crimson Glory

Crimson Velvet

14

Dainty Bess   *Dame Edith Helen*

Diamond Jubilee

Eden Rose
Edina

17

Edith Nellie Perkins   Étoile de Hollande

Ena Harkness

Farandole

19

Frau Karl Druschki

Flaming Sunset

20

Fru Julie Poulsen

Général
Jacqueminot

Geheimrat Duisberg

Frensham

21

Golden Sun

22

Golden Masterpiece

Grande Duchesse Charlotte

Grace de Monaco

23

Grand'mère Jenny
Gruss an Aachen

Innocence   *Elsinore*   *Hanne* 25

Irene of Denmark

Jolie Madame

Josephine Bruce

Konrad Adenauer

27

Perfecta

Kordes Korona
Lilli Marlene

Masquerade

Margo Koster

Marcelle Gret

30

Meteor

Message
Märchenland

31

Mme. Caroline Testout

M. Nathalie Nypels

Michèle Meilland

33

McGredy's Sunset   *Mme. Butterfly*

Mrs. Sam McGredy

Mrs. John Laing

Mrs. Pierre S. Dupont

Orange Triumph

Montezuma

Mojave

Peace

Picture

Piccadilly

Perla de Alcanada

Red
Pinocchio

Yellow Pinocchio

Pink Pinocchio

Pink Peace

39

Poulsen's Grupperose

Poulsen's Pink

Poinsettia   *Poppy*

President
Herbert Hoover

Prelude

42

Queen Elizabeth 43

Cardinal's Hat

Rimosa

Rose Gaujard

Rumba

45

Sarabande

Spek's Yellow

Iceberg

Sutter's Gold

Sundance

Suspense

47

Soraya

Spartan

Super Star

48

Talisman

Tawny Gold

Texas Centennial

49

Toni Lander

Tzigane

50

Tiffany
Tivoli

51

Virgo

52

Yvonne Rabier

Ulrich Brunner

Zambra

53

Aloha

Blaze

Chaplin's Pink

American Pillar

Climbing Goldilocks

54

Excelsa

Danse des Sylphes

Easlea's Golden Rambler

White Dorothy

Dorothy Perkins

Danse de Feu

55

Gloire de Dijon

Gruss an Zabern

Golden Showers

Hiawatha

Heidelberg

High Noon

56

Leverkusen

Maigold

New Dawn

57

Sanders White

Royal Scarlet

Veilchenblau

Tausendschön

Wilhelm Hansmann

58

Rosa alba

Maiden's Blush

Rosa blanda

Rosa canina x
Jacqueminot

Rosa
carolina

Lucy Bertram

Rosa helenae

Rosa foetida Persiana

Rosa hugonis

Rosa moyesii

Rosa multiflora

Rosa moyesii

Nevada

Sparrieshoop

Rosa rubrifolia

Rosa omeiensis
pteracantha

62

Rosa rugosa
Fru Dagmar Hastrup

Pink Grootendorst

F. J. Grootendorst

Stella Polaris

Rustica

Rosa spinosissima hybrida

Frühlingsmorgen

Frühlingsgold

64   *Rosa willmottiae*

Description of the roses

The following alphabetic register gives a description of all the roses depicted in the colour plates. The number against each rose refers to the plate number.

The roses are arranged according to the name of the variety. This is followed by the group to which each rose belongs, e.g. climber, hybrid tea, shrub rose, hybrid perpetual or floribunda. The name of the breeder follows, insofar as this is known, and the year in which it was produced. Finally, the parentage of the rose is given in brackets, again so far as it is known; this is expressed as paternal parent x maternal parent.

The descriptions speak for themselves; it is only necessary to stress that the information on scent must necessarily be vague and where none is given the rose is scentless. Similarly the height data are only approximate; growth may vary significantly according to soil, climate, pruning, manuring and so on.

The colour illustrations of the large-flowered garden roses will be found on plates 6–53, of climbing roses on plates 54–58, and of shrub roses on plates 59–64.

ALAIN *plate 6*
Floribunda
Meilland 1946
[(Guinée x Wilhelm) x Orange Triumph]
Scarlet, semi-double flowers in large clusters. Robust growth with fine, healthy, dark foliage. Above knee height (28 in). Flowers late and over a long period.

ALLGOLD 6
Floribunda
Le Grice 1956
[Goldilocks x Ellinor Le Grice]
Pointed, yellow buds with long sepals; the semi-double, bright golden-yellow flowers are faintly scented and are arranged singly or in loose clusters. Robust, healthy and bushy growth, above knee height (28 in) with dark green leaves. Flowers until far into the autumn. Perhaps the best yellow floribunda rose.

ALOHA 54
Large-flowered climbing rose
Boerner, Jackson and Perkins 1955
[Mercedes Gallart x New Dawn]
Large copper-pink, tightly filled flowers with a beautiful shape and fine scent. Suffers somewhat during rainy periods. Flowers from July to late autumn, when the withered blooms should be removed immediately. Moderate growth to about 6 ft, with beautiful dark green foliage. Can also be planted free-standing as a shrub rose. Only moderate pruning of the short branches after they have flowered.

AMA 6
Floribunda
Kordes 1955
[Obergartner Wiebicke x Independence]
Dark scarlet, semi-double flowers in large erect clusters. Vigorous, healthy growth to about knee height (22–27 in). Long and very late-flowering.

AMERICAN PILLAR 54
Rambler
Dr van Fleet 1902
[(R. *wichuraiana* x R. *setigera*) x a red Hybrid Perpetual]
Clear, carmine single blooms with white centres, in large trusses. Very hardy and long-flowering, but only flowers once. Unusually vigorous growth with thick shoots 9–12 ft long produced in a single summer. Requires plenty of space and frequent thinning out of the old branches right down to the ground.

BACCARA   7
Hybrid tea
Meilland 1956
[Happiness x Independence]
Globular buds opening to give brilliant geranium-red blooms; the flower is finely formed like a bowl, even when fully open, and it lasts very well when cut. No scent. Erect growth to about hip height (30–39 in) and dark foliage. Does best in a greenhouse.

BALLET   7
Hybrid tea
Kordes 1958
[Florex x Karl Herbst]
Large double, scentless blooms, which retain their pure pink colour until they wither. Vigorous growth to above knee height (27 in) and beautiful grey-green foliage.

BELLE BLONDE   8
Hybrid tea
Meilland 1955
[Peace x Lorraine]
Large, well-formed flowers with bright golden-yellow petals which become darker towards the centre. Fragrant and lasts particularly well when cut. Good growth, medium height (19–23 in).

BETTINA   8
Hybrid tea
Meilland 1953
[Peace x (Mme Joseph Perraud x Demain)]
Dark orange-yellow with copper-red veins and shading on the petals. Large, well-filled blooms with a strong scent. Tall, vigorous growth and beautiful, glossy, dark green leaves. Above knee height (27 in). Requires a good, warm sunny position.

BETTY PRIOR   8
Floribunda
Prior 1935
[Kirsten Poulsen x unnamed seedling]
Large umbels of single, cherry-red flowers with pale pink edges. Robust growth to hip height (35 in).

BETTY UPRICHARD   9
Hybrid tea
Alex Dickson 1921
Salmon-pink petals with dark pink to pink on the reverse. Faint scent. A robust rose which flowers profusely over a long period. Up to hip height (35 in).

BLAZE   54
Climber
Kallay 1932
[Paul's Scarlet Climber x Gruss an Teplitz]
Bright scarlet flowers in loose trusses, produced very profusely and often several times in the course of the summer. Resembles Paul's Scarlet Climber, previously much cultivated, but flowers over a longer period.

BUCCANEER   9
Hybrid tea
Swim 1952
[Geheimrat Duisberg x (Max Krause x Capt. Thomas)]
Attractive medium-sized buttercup-yellow flowers with a marked scent. Very tall growth to above hip height (35–45 in) with glossy, dark green foliage.

BURNET ROSE—see *Rosa spinosissima*

CARDINAL'S HAT (RODHATTE—also trans-   44
lated as RED RIDING HOOD)
Floribunda
D. Poulsen 1911
[Mme Norbert Levavasseur x Richmond]
A clear, cherry-red with a faint bluish sheen, which means that this rose will clash with other red roses. Medium-sized, semi-double flowers in trusses; it is hardy, easily satisfied and tolerates shade. This rose is included because it is a particularly old variety suitable for enclosed town gardens and in general where conditions are difficult. Robust growth to above knee height (27 in).

CHAMPS ELYSEES   10
Hybrid tea
Meilland 1957
[Monique x Happiness]

Rich red with soft, velvety shading. Large well-shaped flowers, but only a faint scent. Vigorous growth with upright stems. Above knee height (27–35 in).

CHAPLIN'S PINK CLIMBER   54
Climber
Chaplin 1928
[Paul's Scarlet Climber x American Pillar]
Clear pink, semi-double flowers in clusters; stamens golden-yellow. Very robust growth with shoots 6–9 ft long. Flowers now and again after the main flowering in July. Lasts very well when cut.

CHARLES BONNET   11
Hybrid perpetual
Bonnet 1884
Dark rose-pink flowers with a fragrant scent. Robust growth to a height of about 35 in. Flowers in mid-summer.

CHINATOWN   11
Floribunda shrub
N. D. Poulsen 1963
[Columbine x Claire Grammersdorff]
Warm, bright yellow flowers with slightly fringed edges to the petals. Pleasant scent and glossy, dark green leaves. Very robust growth to above hip height (40–45 in). Flowers until late autumn. Requires plenty of space and should be only lightly pruned. Can be grown on a wall as an espalier.

CHRISTOPHER STONE   11
Hybrid tea
Robinson 1934
[Etoile de Hollande x Hortulanus Budde]
Large, well-filled, dark red flowers with a fine and very strong scent. Growth is moderate and the foliage fresh green; up to hip height (27–35 in).

CHRYSLER IMPERIAL   13
Hybrid tea
Lammerts 1952
[Charlotte Armstrong x Mirandy]
Dark blood-red with lighter tones. A beautifully shaped double rose which does well and has a strong, pleasant scent. Large, dark green leaves and vigorous growth almost to hip height (31 in).

CIRCUS   12
Floribunda
Swim 1955
[Fandango x Pinocchio]
Variously coloured in delicate shades of yellow, pink, salmon-pink and pure red. The well-filled, medium-sized flowers are in beautiful large clusters framed by fine, glossy, dark green leaves. Marked scent. Low, compact growth to about knee height (23 in).

CLIMBING GOLDILOCKS   54
Climbing bouquet rose
Boerner, Jackson and Perkins 1952
This climbing sport of the profusely flowering, yellow floribunda rose, Goldilocks, produces well-shaped flowers which last until far into the autumn. Sometimes a little difficult to get going and it is best to pick off the first flowers; prune the branches well back on first year plants so as to get a good growth of shoots from the base. With good nutrient and regular removal of withered flowers, this rose may reach a height of 6–9 ft.

COLUMBINE   12
Floribunda
S. Poulsen 1956
[Danish Gold x Frensham]
Pale yellow flushed with red. Delicate, well-formed flowers of hybrid tea-type in loose clusters. Unusually fragrant for a floribunda rose. Vigorous growth to about 23–27 in. Flowers until late summer.

CONCERTO   12
Floribunda
Meilland 1953
[Alain x Floradora]
Clear, glowing scarlet petals. Medium-sized, semi-double flowers in loose trusses. Bushy growth to below knee height (15–20 in), with dark green foliage.

COPPER ROSE—see ROSA RUBRIFOLIA

CRICRI　　　　　　　　　　*14*
Miniature rose
Meilland 1958
[(Alain x Independence) x Perla de Alcanada]
Elegant, small, salmon-pink flowers which are produced all over the tiny, compact, low-growing plant. An attractive and graceful plant which only grows to a height of about 12 in.

CRIMSON GLORY　　　　　　*14*
Hybrid tea
Kordes 1935
[Katharine Kordes seedling x W. E. Chaplin]
Large, full, dark red flowers with velvety shading and a strong pleasant scent. The flowers become bluish as they fade. Vigorous, compact growth, to about knee height (23 in). Very susceptible to disease.

CRIMSON VELVET　　　　　　*14*
Floribunda
O. Sønderhousen 1960
[Cocorico x Hanne]
Large, single, blood-red flowers with unusually beautiful colour tones. Vigorous, upright growth. Height about 15–19 in.

CYNTHIA BROOKE　　　　　　*13*
Hybrid tea
McGredy 1942
[Le Progrès x (Mme Mélanie Soupert x Le Progrès)]
A warm, apricot-yellow colour and large, characteristically spherical, tightly filled blooms, which last well and have a fine scent. Robust, bushy growth with leathery leaves. About knee height (23 in).

DAINTY BESS　　　　　　　*15*
Hybrid tea
Archer 1925
[Ophelia x K. of K.]
Pure pale-pink with beautiful single flowers and elegantly shaped buds. Very vigorous growth and fine foliage. Height 23–31 in.

DAME EDITH HELEN　　　　　*15*
Hybrid tea
A. Dickson 1926

Large, well-filled, pink to salmon-pink flowers with a good scent. Growth moderate, scarcely reaching to knee height (19 in).

DANSE DES SYLPHES　　　　　*55*
Large-flowered climber
Mallerin 1957
[Danse de Feu x Toujours]
Bright orange-red, full and plump blooms in loose clusters. Now and then it flowers right into the autumn after the main flowering. Moderate growth with shoots up to 6–9 ft. Only the short branches that have produced flowers should be pruned.

DANSE DE FEU　　　　　　　*55*
Large-flowered climber
Mallerin 1954
[Paul's Scarlet Climber x *R. multiflora* seedling]
Full, orange scarlet blooms with a marked scent. Flowers several times throughout the summer and tolerates a certain amount of rain. Growth moderate with shoots up to 6–9 ft, and beautiful foliage.

DIAMOND JUBILEE　　　　　　*16*
Hybrid tea
Jackson and Perkins 1947
[Maréchal Niel x Feu Pernet Ducher]
Large, full, strongly scented flowers, yellow in colour which may change to pale orange. Dark green leathery foliage and vigorous growth up to knee height (25 in).

DOROTHY PERKINS　　　　　　*55*
Rambler
Jackson and Perkins 1901
[*R. wichuraiana* x Mme Gabriel Luizet]
Small, pink, double flowers with a pale salmon-pink sheen produced in large, compact trusses on long, slender green canes; foliage pale green. Flowers in July, but only once. The canes grow to 12–15 ft long and those that have flowered should be removed or thinned out immediately so as to give the new shoots light and air. One of the first valuable varieties among the so-called Wichuraiana hybrids (see page 56); it appeared at the turn of the century and is still reckoned among

the most beautiful of the climbing roses.

EASLEA'S GOLDEN RAMBLER   55
Large-flowered climber
Easlea 1932
Bright yellow with a pink tinge; beautiful buds
and full flowers in small clusters. Very attractive,
dark green, glossy foliage. Only flowers once.
Vigorous growth with stems up to 9–12 ft long.

EDEN ROSE   17
Hybrid tea
Meilland 1950
[Peace x Signora]
Petals deep pink with paler reverse. Very full,
beautifully shaped flowers with a fine scent.
Robust, erect growth and attractive dark green
foliage. Above hip height (39 in).

EDINA   17
Hybrid tea
Dobbie 1934
Very beautifully shaped buds and half-opened
flowers which are white with a pale pink flush.
Fragrant. Vigorous growth to about 23–27 in.

EDITH NELLIE PERKINS   18
Hybrid tea
A. Dickson 1928
Pale salmon-pink, tightly filled blooms of elegant
shape, the reverse orient-red, flushed orange.
Healthy, vigorous growth to above knee height
(27 in).

ELSINORE   25
Floribunda
R. V. Lindquist 1958
[Floradora x Pinocchio]
Semi-double scarlet flowers in large, loose trusses.
Robust growth. Similar to Moulin Rouge. Height
about 31 in.

ENA HARKNESS   19
Hybrid tea
Norman 1946
[Crimson Glory x Southport]
Clear, bright scarlet flowers of exceptionally
beautiful form, which are particularly good for
cutting. The colour persists until the petals fall.

Faint scent and long stems. Robust growth and
pretty foliage. Above knee height (27–31 in).

ETOILE DE HOLLANDE   18
Hybrid tea
H. A. Verschuren 1919
[General MacArthur x Hadley]
A rich, dark red colour which persists; well-
filled blooms with a very strong scent. Vigorous
growth, slightly pendulous flowers, which will be
less pronounced if the shoots are cut back after
each flowering. Flowers over a long period, right
into the autumn. About knee height (25 in).

EXCELSA   55
Rambler
Walsh 1909
Small but full, shiny, bright red flowers in large
clusters. Long, pale green canes and pale foliage.
Flowers only once, but still one of the best ramblers.
Growth robust with canes up to 12–15 ft long.
Drastic pruning of old shoots right down to the
ground, immediately after flowering, is very
rewarding. Also called Red Dorothy Perkins.

FARANDOLE   19
Floribunda
Meilland 1959
[(Goldilocks x Moulin Rouge) x (Goldilocks x
Fashion)]
Pale orange-red, semi-double flowers in broad
trusses. No scent. Broad, compact growth,
scarcely to knee height (19–23 in). Tolerates bad
weather and is very resistant to disease.

F. J. GROOTENDORST   63
Shrub rose
Grootendorst 1918
[*R. rugosa rubra* x Mme Norbert Levavasseur]
Small, bright red double flowers resembling
carnations, carried in large trusses, those around
the edge being neatly serrated. Stiff, upright
growth to about shoulder height.

FLAMING SUNSET   20
Hybrid tea
Eddie 1947
[Sport of McGredy's Sunset]
Deep orange-red with yellow edges to the petals.

Large, shapely but scentless flowers. Moderate growth to knee height (19 in) and attractive reddish foliage.

FRAU KARL DRUSCHKI   20
Hybrid tea
Lambert 1900
[Merveille de Lyon x Mme Caroline Testout]
Buds pale pink, open flowers dazzling white, shapely, large and well-filled but without scent. Late-flowering. Vigorous, tall growth to about hip height (39 in). The very coarse foliage is sometimes attacked by fungus. Also known under the name Snow Queen.

FRENSHAM   21
Floribunda
Norman 1946
[A floribunda seedling x Crimson Glory]
Bright deep scarlet, semi-double flowers in large clusters. Vigorous, growth to above hip height (39–55 ins), almost forming a bush. Very suitable for low, flowering hedges. Hardy and continuous flowering.

FRÜHLINGSGOLD   64
Shrub rose
W. Kordes 1937
[Joanna Hill x *R. spinosissima hispida*]
Growth similar to that of Frühlingsmorgen, but with large, pale yellow, semi-double flowers, up to about 6 ft.

FRÜHLINGSMORGEN   64
Shrub rose
W. Kordes 1941
[(E. G. Hill x Cathrine Kordes) x *R. spinosissima altaica*]
A really delightful shrub rose with long, over-hanging branches covered during May–June with large, single, delicate pink flowers with yellowish centres and red-brown stamens – a remarkably lovely colour combination. The bush, which reaches nearly to the height of a man, should be planted in a place where it has plenty of space to develop.

FRU JULIE POULSEN (POULSEN'S DELIGHT)
Floribunda

S. Poulsen 1948
[Else Poulsen x a seedling]
Large, almost single, delicate pink flowers, with yellowish shading, produced in graceful, slender trusses. With its reddish young leaves and stems this plant is a charming and characteristic floribunda. An exceptionally beautiful Danish rose which is far too little known and used. Lasts well as a cut flower. About knee height (23 in).

GEHEIMRAT DUISBERG (Golden Rapture)   21
Hybrid tea
Kordes 1933
[Rapture x Julien Potin]
Pure pale yellow, somewhat darker yellow in late summer. Elegant, tightly filled, delicately shaped flowers with pointed buds. Attractive, quite low growth – below knee height (17 in). An excellent rose for cutting and forces well.

GENERAL JACQUEMINOT   21
Hybrid perpetual
Rousel 1853
[A seedling from Gloire des Rosomanes]
Large, globular well-filled scarlet flowers. Very sweet-scented. Tall, vigorous growth to over hip height (48 in). Should not be pruned too much.

GLOIRE DE DIJON   56
Climbing tea rose
Jacotot 1853
[An unknown tea rose x Souvenir de la Malmaison]
Beautiful, full, strongly scented flowers which are golden-pink to pale yellow. Unsurpassed by any other rose within its colour range. If planted on a south wall, it will flower very early – often at the end of May – and go on until right into the autumn. It also flowers well on a north wall, but then the withered blooms must be removed regularly and the plant kept well watered and manured. Stems up to 9–12 ft.

GOLDEN SUN   22
Hybrid tea
Kordes 1957
[(Walter Bentley x Condesa de Sástago) x Spek's Yellow]
Shapely, deep lemon-yellow flowers, several

growing together in clusters on long, stiff shoots. Vigorous growth to above knee height (29 in) with green foliage. Long-flowering.

GOLDEN MASTERPIECE 23

Hybrid tea

Boerner, Jackson and Perkins 1953

[Mandalay x Spek's Yellow]

Very beautiful, long buds which open into large, bright, well-filled, lemon-yellow flowers. Distinctive scent. Vigorous, upright growth to above knee height (29 in) with glossy, dark green foliage. Good for forcing.

GOLDEN SHOWERS 56

Climber

Lammerts 1957

[Charlotte Armstrong x Capt. Thomas]

This new climbing rose from the U.S.A. has very beautiful, slender buds and large, semi-double golden-yellow flowers with a distinctive scent. After the main flowering in June, new flowers are produced regularly until far into the autumn. Growth is moderate and the stems reach a length of 6–9 ft.

GOLDILOCKS 54

Floribunda

Boerner, Jackson and Perkins 1945

[A seedling x Doubloons]

Medium-sized, full, globular, golden-yellow to cream-yellow flowers in loose clusters. Compact, low, bushy growth, below knee height (17 in). See also Climbing Goldilocks.

GRACE DE MONACO 23

Hybrid tea

Meilland 1956

[Peace x Michèle Meilland]

With its beautiful, pure pale-pink colour and large double flowers this is one of the very best roses. Very fragrant. Strong, upright growth to above knee height (29 in) with glossy green leaves.

GRANDE DUCHESSE CHARLOTTE 23

Hybrid tea

Ketten Brothers 1942

Bright orange-red with a little yellow at the base of the petals. Very large, longish flowers. Vigorous

growth to about knee height (20–23 in).

GRAND'MERE JENNY 24

Hybrid tea

Meilland 1950

[Peace x Signora]

The principal colour is a beautiful pure yellow, but the edges of the petals are suffused with pink, varying somewhat according to season. Faint scent, very vigorous growth to about 31 in. Glossy green leaves.

GRUSS AN AACHEN 24

Polyantha

Geduldig 1909

[Frau Karl Druschki x Franz Deeger]

Pale pink shading to yellow. Large, double, scented flowers in loose clusters. Flowers very profusely and grows low and spreading (15 in).

GRUSS AN ZABERN 56

Climber

P. Lambert 1904

[Euphrosine x Mme Oscar Ferencz]

This old *R. multiflora* hybrid is still one of the best white climbing roses. It has large clusters of pure white, strongly scented double flowers. Robust growth with canes about 6–9 ft long.

HANNE 25

Hybrid tea

O. Sønderhousen 1959

[Ena Harkness x Peace]

A magnificent, full rose with slender, shapely buds and a bright, deep red colour which persists until the petals fall. Very strong fragrance. Good growth and beautiful foliage. Height 23–27 in. Without doubt one of the best of the scented red roses.

HEIDELBERG 56

Climber or shrub rose

Kordes 1958

[Minna Kordes x Floradora]

Very beautiful, well-formed buds and scented, blood-red double blooms in small clusters. Flowers profusely, right on into the autumn. Growth is vigorous and upright, and it is well suited to cultivation as an espalier on a wall or wooden fence, also as a free-standing bush in among low-growing roses. The withered flowers should be removed regularly and pruning restricted, in general, to a moderate cutting back of the short flowering branches with some rejuvenation every few years.

HIAWATHA 56
Climber
M. H. Walsh 1905
[Crimson Rambler x Paul's Carmine Pillar]
This old rose is included on account of its very distinctive appearance. It has numerous, small, single, dark-red, white-centred flowers, several together in large clusters, with tufts of yellow stamens. Flowers last well and continue over a long period. Vigorous growth with canes of 6–9 ft or more under favourable conditions.

HIGH NOON 56
Climber
Lammerts 1946
[Soeur Thérèse x Captain Thomas]
Large, clear, dark yellow, semi-double flowers. Long-flowering and fragrant. Leathery, glossy foliage and moderate growth with canes about 6 ft long.

ICEBERG 46
Floribunda
W. Kordes 1958
[Robin Hood x Virgo]
Dazzling, pure white, delicately shaped flowers in large, loose clusters. Faint scent. Very handsome, glossy foliage and graceful, tall growth up to hip height (35 in).

INNOCENCE 25
Hybrid tea
Chaplin 1921
Large, pure white, semi-double flowers with red stamens which give the flowers a particularly beautiful appearance. Vigorous and upright growth – up to hip height (35 in). Looks particularly well among perennials.

IRENE OF DENMARK 26
Floribunda
S. Poulsen 1951

[Mrs W. H. Cutbush x Edina]
Very finely shaped, white flowers, rather like small gardenias. Thrives and flowers profusely until far into late summer. Faint scent. Very attractive, glossy green foliage; generally speaking, the growth is elegant and graceful, but broad and low – below knee height (20 in).

JAPANESE ROSE—see ROSA RUGOSA

JOLIE MADAME 27
Hybrid tea
Meilland 1958
[(Independence x Happiness) x Better Times]
Medium-sized, pale vermilion double flowers in small clusters. Slightly fragrant. Sturdy erect growth to about knee height (20–23 in). A good rose for forcing.

JOSEPHINE BRUCE 27
Hybrid tea
Bees 1952
[Crimson Glory x Madge Whipp]
Large, full, finely scented, dark velvety-crimson flowers which keep well. Dark green foliage and vigorous bushy growth up to at least knee height (27–31 in).

KONRAD ADENAUER 27
Hybrid tea
Tantau 1954
[Crimson Glory x Hans Verschuren]
Clear, dark red globular, double flowers which keep very well and have a pleasant scent. Handsome, light green foliage and moderate growth to about knee height (23 in).

KORONA 29
Floribunda
Kordes 1953
[Obergartner Wiebecke x Independence]
Glowing orange-scarlet, semi-double flowers in large trusses. Slightly fragrant. Robust growth with long shoots from the base up to above knee height (29 in). Requires only light pruning.

LABRADOR ROSE—see ROSA BLANDA

LEVERKUSEN 57
Large-flowered climber
Kordes 1955

[*R. Kordesii* x Golden Glow]
Semi-double golden-yellow blooms on long shoots which flower right through the summer until late into the autumn. The leaves are glossy and dark green and free from disease. Sturdy growth with vigorous stems 6–9 ft long.

LILLI MARLENE 29
Floribunda
Kordes 1959
[Our Princess x Rudolph Timm]
Semi-double, almost spherical, deep blood-red flowers in large trusses. The colour is unusually beautiful and it persists from when the flower opens until it withers. Flowers profusely until late summer. Faintly scented. Moderate, compact growth (23–27 in) with handsome, abundant foliage.

LUCY BERTRAM—see ROSA EGLANTERIA

MCGREDY'S SUNSET 34
Hybrid tea
McGredy 1936
[Margaret McGredy x Mabel Morse]
Petals with warm yellow bases shading to scarlet above; petal edges pale yellow. A little loose and open, with a distinct scent. Handsome, bronze-red foliage and moderate growth to about knee height (23 in).

MME BUTTERFLY 34
Hybrid tea
Hill 1918
[Sport from Ophelia]
Medium-sized, well-filled, shapely, dark salmon-pink flowers; fragrant and carried on long stems. Strong upright growth to above knee height (29 in). A good variety for cutting.

MME CAROLINE TESTOUT 32
Hybrid tea
Pernet Ducher 1890
[Mme de Tartas x Lady Mary Fitzwilliam]
Tight-filled, spherical, pure pink flowers, somewhat darker in the centre. Distinctive scent. One of the older roses which is still much planted, because it is easily satisfied; it tolerates a little shade and poor weather conditions. Goes on flowering right into the autumn. Strong growth, up to hip height (37 in).

MAIDEN'S BLUSH 59
Shrub rose
This is one of the old, highly valued cultivated roses; it was produced by crossing *R. alba* and *R. centifolia*. In its growth and profusion of flowers it resembles the ordinary *R. alba,* but the blooms are a charming pale pink colour with a slightly yellowish tint. Wonderfully fragrant. It should be planted up against a wall in a warm sunny position.

MAIGOLD 57
Climber
Kordes 1953
[Poulsen's Pink x Frühlingstag]
Very large, distinctive, warm amber-yellow blooms with a strong scent. Flowers early but will go on doing so for a long time if the withered blooms are cut off regularly. Large thorns and very robust growth with stems up to 9–15 ft.

MARCELLE GRET 30
Hybrid tea
Meilland 1947
[Peace x Princess Beatrix]
A handsome rose with golden-yellow flowers on strong, stiff stems. Slightly fragrant, vigorous upright growth to above knee height (27 in) and glossy, dark green foliage.

MÄRCHENLAND 31
Floribunda
Tantau 1951
[Swantje x Hamburg]
Pale pink with faint, dark salmon-pink shading. Semi-double flowers in large clusters. Long-flowering and lasts extremely well. Very handsome, glossy foliage and good, healthy growth up to hip height (37 in).

MARGO KOSTER 30
Polyantha
D. A. Koster 1931
[Sport from Dick Koster]
Small, round, salmon-pink flowers in trusses. Known under the popular name of Sunbeam, it

is also found in a red and a pure white form. Glossy foliage and bushy, branching growth to below knee height.

MASQUERADE 30
Floribunda
Boerner, Jackson and Perkins 1949
[Goldilocks x Holiday]
Buds bright yellow turning to pink and pure red – an attractive play of colours which corresponds with the name. Very large trusses with a delicate scent. Handsome, dark foliage and vigorous, bushy growth to about knee height (27 in).

MESSAGE 31
Hybrid tea
Meilland 1956
[Virgo x Peace]
Pure white with a faint greenish tinge which accentuates the whiteness. Graceful flowers, slender in shape and slightly fragrant. Moderate growth to about knee height (23 in). Particularly suitable for cutting. Also known as White Knight.

METEOR 31
Floribunda
Kordes 1958
[Feurio x Gertrud Westphal]
Brilliant, intense cinnabar-red which is very striking from a distance but may clash with other roses in the vicinity. The flat, but tightly packed single flowers grow in small clusters and are very persistent both on the bush and also when cut. No scent. Low and compact, bushy growth to knee height with light green foliage.

MEVROUW NATHALIE NYPELS 33
Polyantha
Leenders 1919
[Orléans Rose x (Comt. du Cayla x *R. foetida bicolor*)]
Small, beautifully shaped, pale pink flowers in loose clusters. Graceful and elegant growth with handsome foliage. Late flowering. Moderate growth to about knee height.

MICHELE MEILLAND 33
Hybrid tea
Meilland 1945

[Joanna Hill x Peace]
Shapely, whitish pink flowers with salmon-pink shading, which last well when cut. Fragrant. Tall, robust growth with the flowers on long stiff stems. Up to below hip height (31 in).

MOJAVE 36
Hybrid tea
Swim 1956
[Charlotte Armstrong x Signora]
Characteristic dark orange flowers with red shading and veining. The flowers are a little loose and the foliage is a glossy dark green. Vigorous growth to about hip height (27–38 in).

MONTEZUMA 36
Hybrid tea
Swim 1955
[Fandango x Floradora]
Large, spherical, salmon-pink flowers on long, stiff stems with handsome dark green foliage. Slightly fragrant. A characteristic and beautiful rose for cutting. Robust growth to about hip height (30–45 in).

MRS JOHN LAING 35
Hybrid perpetual
Bennett 1887
[Seedling from François Michelon]
Handsome buds and pale, silky, well-filled, pink flowers with a very pleasant scent. Very robust, tall growth to above hip height (40 in). One of the most valuable of the older roses which should still be planted. But it needs plenty of space, although a few can be planted together to form a large, free-standing bush.

MRS PIERRE S. DU PONT 35
Hybrid tea
Mallerin 1929
[(Ophelia x Rayon d'Or) x ((Ophelia x (Constance x Souv. de Claudius Pernet)]
A pure golden-yellow colour, and very shapely, tightly packed flowers. Slightly fragrant. Handsome glossy foliage and moderate growth to about knee height (23 in). One of the best roses for profusion and length of flowering.

MRS SAM MCGREDY   35

Hybrid tea

McGredy 1929

[(Donald MacDonald x Golden Emblem) x (a
seedling x The Queen Alexandra Rose)]

Large, slender, scarlet coppery-orange flowers –
a characteristic blend of colours with a good,
distinctive scent. The shoots and leaves have their
own coppery-red colour which goes well with the
flowers. Moderate growth to above knee height
(27 in).

NEVADA   61

Shrub rose

Dot 1927

[La Giralda x *R. moyesii fargesii*]

Very large, single or loosely packed flowers, pale
pink at first and pure white when fully open, the
centres of the flowers with large tufts of golden-
yellow stamens, giving a beautiful effect. The first
flowering in June is very profuse, forming lovely
garlands of slightly arched, overhanging branches
with handsome, pale green foliage; it also goes
on flowering until the first frosts. This variety,
which reaches a height of 4½–6 ft is one of our most
valuable roses and it should be planted with
plenty of space around it; it is also handsome when
grown up against a wall as an espalier.

NEW DAWN   57

Climber

Dreer 1930

[Sport from Dr W. van Fleet]

Large, shapely and full, delicate pink flowers in
very large clusters. Healthy, vigorous growth
with stems up to 9–12 ft long, and handsome,
glossy foliage. It flowers several times during the
course of the summer, in contrast to Dr W. van
Fleet which it resembles in all other respects.

ORANGE TRIUMPH   36

Floribunda

Kordes 1937

[Eva x Solarium]

Several small, pure orange-red flowers in large
trusses. No scent. Flowers very late but continues
to do so for a long time. Vigorous growth to above

knee height (24–40 in).

PEACE   37

Hybrid tea

Shrub rose

Meilland 1945

[Joanna Hill x (Charles P. Kilham x *R. foetida
bicolor* seedling) x (C. P. Kilham x Margaret
McGredy)]

Pale yellow (sometimes dark yellow) with pink
shading towards the petal tips. Very large, tightly
packed flowers which last a long time, but with
only a faint scent. Robust, healthy, tall growth
with very handsome glossy foliage. Above hip
height (40–55 in). Requires only light pruning.
Other names: Gioia, Gloria Dei, Mme A. Meilland.

PERFECTA   28

Hybrid tea

Kordes 1957

[Spek's Yellow x Karl Herbst]

Petals salmon-pink with pure pink on the outer
edges which are reflexed; petal bases yellow.
When half open this is perhaps the most elegant
and perfectly formed full rose, but it is somewhat
sensitive to rain and cold, windy weather. Faint
scent; handsome, glossy foliage and tall, robust
growth to above knee height (29 in). The flowers
last well when cut.

PERLA DE ALCANADA   38

Miniature rose

Dot 1945

[Perle des Rouges x *R. roulettii*]

Small, elegant, scarlet double flowers in loose
clusters. The whole plant is small and doll-like.
Can be grown in pots but is not suitable for use
amongst other roses. 8–12 in high. Requires sun
and a light, warm soil.

PERSIAN YELLOW—see ROSA FOETIDA

PICCADILLY   38

Hybrid tea

McGredy 1959

[McGredy's Yellow x Karl Herbst]

Golden-yellow with bright red shading. Faint
scent. Healthy, vigorous growth to above knee

height (27 in), and handsome, reddish or dark green, glossy foliage.

PICTURE 38
Hybrid tea
McGredy 1932
Elegant, slender, pure pink flowers. Dark glossy foliage. Moderate, quite low growth – about knee height (23 in). A very healthy rose with good late summer flowering.

PINK GROOTENDORST 63
Shrub rose
Grootendorst 1923
[Sport from F. J. Grootendorst]
Small, tight, double, carnation-like, salmon-pink flowers in large trusses. Stiff, upright growth to about hip height.

PINK PEACE 39
Hybrid tea
Meilland 1959
[(Peace x Monique) x (Peace x Mrs John Laing)]
The deep pink colour and the wonderful old-fashioned rose scent are derived from Mrs John Laing. The handsome growth, fine foliage and very large flowers are characteristics inherited from Peace. A healthy, attractive and robust rose, which is particularly good for cutting. Up to hip height.

PINOCCHIO 39
Floribunda
Kordes 1940
[Eva x Geheimrat Duisberg]
Warm, yellowish-pink flowers, not particularly large but very shapely and firm. Flowers in loose clusters. It is long-flowering and lasts very well. Compact, bushy, low growth – about 20 in. Suitable for forcing and as a cut flower. Also occurs in a pink and in a pure red variety. Alternative name, Rosenmärchen.

POINSETTIA 41
Hybrid tea
Howard & Smith 1938
[(Mrs J. D. Eisele x Vaterland) x J. C. Thornton]
Large, well-filled, bright scarlet flowers like those of Poinsettia, whence its name. Robust growth

to above knee height (27 in). Only thrives really well in a warm position open to the sun and is better in the greenhouse.

POPPY 41
Floribunda
O. Sønderhousen 1960
[Cocorico x Geranium Red]
Large, almost single flowers in large trusses; bright poppy-red colour. Healthy, vigorous growth to above knee height (23–27 in).

POULSEN'S BEDDER (Grupperose) 40
Floribunda
S. Poulsen 1948
[Orléans Rose x Talisman]
Clear pink with a faint yellowish sheen. Semi-double flowers in small clusters. Very healthy and long-flowering; pale bronze foliage. Vigorous, upright growth to about knee height.

POULSEN'S PINK 40
Floribunda
S. Poulsen 1939
[Seedling from Golden Salmon]
Pale pink with yellowish shading towards the centre of the flower. Semi-double flowers in small trusses and pale green foliage. Tall, vigorous and upright growth to above knee height (29 in).

PRELUDE 42
Hybrid tea
Meilland 1955
[(Fantastique x Ampère) x (Charles P. Kilham x Capucine Chambard)]
Pale lavender-blue – a tone which is very unusual in roses and which is not always appreciated by rose lovers. Fragrant. Moderate growth with handsome foliage; about 23 in tall.

PRESIDENT HERBERT HOOVER 42
Hybrid tea
Coddington 1930
[Sensation x Souvenir de Claudius Pernet]
A beautiful golden-yellow with fiery red shading which later changes to dark pink. The slender and finely scented flowers are carried on unusually long stems, so this variety is particularly good for cutting. Handsome, glossy foliage and very

robust growth to about hip height (30–35 in).

QUEEN ELIZABETH (THE QUEEN ELIZABETH
ROSE)   43
Floribunda, hybrid tea-type
Lammerts 1954
[Charlotte Armstrong x Floradora]
A clear pink colour which is unusually persistent.
The medium-sized, beautifully formed and
slightly scented double flowers are carried a few
at a time in handsome, very long-stemmed
clusters. Almost thornless, erect, robust growth
to above hip height (50 in). Requires plenty of
space but only light pruning.

RIMOSA   45
Floribunda
Meilland 1959
[Goldilocks x Perla de Montserrat]
Bright canary-yellow, semi-double flowers in
loose clusters. Low, bushy growth and handsome
fresh green foliage, which shows up well against
the yellow flowers. About knee height (20–23 in).

ROSA ALBA (WHITE ROSE)   59
Shrub rose
This beautiful, old-fashioned rose flowers early
in June, producing cascades of snow-white,
scented, semi-double blooms – but it has only one
flowering. It is scarcely a botanical species,
though possibly a hybrid between *R. gallica* and
R. corymbifera. The historic White Rose of York
is a variety of *R. alba*. The bush has characteristic
grey-green foliage and is easily satisfied regarding
soil, although it flowers best in rich soil.

ROSA BLANDA, LABRADOR ROSE   59
Shrub rose
Native to North America. A very hardy, slightly
coarse shrub rose, about 6 ft tall, which is well-
suited for forming a shelter hedge round the garden
of a country cottage. Single, pink flowers with
yellow stamens and bright red hips.

ROSA CANINA X JACQUEMINOT   59
Shrub rose
Kiese & Co. 1910
Single or semi-double, bright red flowers. Robust
growth to $4\frac{1}{2}$–6 ft, with handsome, glossy foliage.

Large orange-red hips.

ROSA CAROLINA   59
Shrub rose
A very easily satisfied and healthy North American
species with pure pink single flowers in tight
clusters; the bright red hips appear after flowering
(see colour plate 1). Glossy, dark green leaves and
broad, compact growth up to 55 in, with suckers.
An excellent bush rose for forming a dense hedge
with, for example, *R. virginiana* and *R. rugosa*.

ROSA EGLANTERIA "LUCY BERTRAM", Apple
Rose   59
Shrub rose
The species *R. eglanteria* grows wild in many places
in Europe. It is called the Apple Rose because the
young shoots and leaves give off a very fine and
pleasant scent of ripe apples, particularly when
rubbed or after rain. The bushes can be grown
to form a hedge or thicket as cover for a slope, and
they provide suitable nesting sites for small birds.
The hybrid, Lucy Bertram, has large, single,
bright red flowers followed by very large coral-
red hips.

ROSA FOETIDA PERSIANA   60
Shrub rose
This old shrub rose which comes from western
Asia has full, brilliant canary-yellow flowers.
R. foetida has provided very important material
for hybridisation, in that it indirectly brought its
"yellow blood" to our most beautiful yellow roses,
such as Peace, Spek's Yellow, President Herbert
Hoover and others. Persian Yellow, which grows
to a good 3 ft, thrives best in light soil in a sheltered
sunny position.

ROSA HELENAE   60
Shrub rose
A very vigorous wild rose from China which
produces slender overhanging shoots, up to
9–12 ft long, with handsome glossy dark green
leaves. The flowers are creamy-yellow at first,
but become pure white when fully open; they are
carried in medium-sized trusses and have an
unusually fine, aromatic scent. The small attractive hips are orange-red. *R. helenae* may become

frosted in a bad winter, but *R. helenae* hybrids, of which there are several forms, such as Aksel Olsen's yellow-flowered variety, Lykkefund, are more hardy.

ROSA HUGONIS   *60*
Shrub rose
This very beautiful shrub rose was brought to Europe about the turn of the century by the missionary Hugh Scollan. At the beginning of June – or even in late May – the whole bush is covered with a mass of pale sulphur-yellow, single flowers which look particularly attractive against its delicate fern-like foliage. The bush, which is only slightly thorny, reaches a good 6 ft and should be grown free-standing to show its elegant and graceful shape. The old shoots should be pruned right down to the ground once a year.

ROSA MOYESII   *61*
Shrub rose
Hemsley & Wilson 1927
A robust rose from Tibet, up to 9 ft tall, with strong, sharp thorns and finely pinnate leaves. The blood-red, single flowers appear in June and the long, curved main branches form graceful arches. After flowering, the plant produces long, flask-shaped, bright red hips which last a long time and are very decorative throughout most of the winter. As the bush has a tendency to become somewhat thin below, it is a good idea to plant low-growing plants around its base, e.g. *Hypericum* Hidcote, *R. rugosa* Stella Polaris, *Berberis polyantha* which blend well with it.

ROSA MULTIFLORA   *61*
A very vigorous bush rose from China and Japan. It produces numerous 3-foot long, fresh green shoots which soon form a tangled wilderness. The small white flowers, each with a tuft of yellow stamens, are carried in tight clusters. The attractive, orange-red hips are about the size of a pea (see colour plate 1). This wild rose has provided important material for hybridisation, and many beautiful climbers and bouquet roses contain *R. multiflora* blood. Although not particularly suitable for ordinary gardens, this rose can be used in extensive grounds to produce living hedges and as cover for slopes.

ROSA OMEIENSIS PTERACANTHA   *62*
Shrub rose
The special beauty of this rose lies in the very large, flat, red thorns, which – particularly on the young shoots – give it an unusually handsome appearance. It produces small, white flowers and red hips which later turn black. It can be used as a hedge around the garden – perhaps to keep unwelcome visitors away. N.B. The white flowers shown in the plate should have four petals instead of five (the yellow has five).

ROSA RUBRIFOLIA, COPPER ROSE   *62*
Shrub rose
This tall shrub rose (6 ft) is first distinguished by the elegant growth of its handsome, red-brown foliage with a bluish sheen. After the dark pink flowers have withered, it is then covered with round glossy red hips. It is perhaps our most beautiful shrub rose, even in winter, when the fine, reddish branches and numerous pendant hips are seen against a background of freshly fallen snow.

ROSA RUGOSA, Fru Dagmar Hastrup   *63*
Shrub rose
A native of eastern Siberia and Japan, this is one of the most easily satisfied and hardy shrub roses. It is particularly suitable for growing in poor, sandy soil along the coast. It spreads rapidly by means of underground runners and forms a dense thicket. The leaves are dark green and wrinkled. The thorns are large and sharp, shaped like a brush. The wild species may reach a height of 6 ft whereas the varieties only grow to $3-4\frac{1}{2}$ ft. This species has violet flowers and, in autumn, large orange-red hips and handsome yellow-red foliage.

ROSA RUSTICA   *63*
Shrub rose
Barbier 1929
[Mme Ed. Herriot x Harison Yellow]
Vigorous growth up to shoulder height with long, graceful, arching branches which bear large,

golden semi-double flowers. It should be planted free-standing to show it at its best, but it can also be used on sunny banks.

ROSA SPINOSISSIMA, SCOTS or BURNET ROSE
64

Shrub rose

Grows wild along the coasts and in the hedgerows of Britain. Slender branches and low, compact, whippy growth up to at least knee height. Spreads rapidly by suckers and has single, pale yellow flowers and brownish-black hips. *R. spinosissima altaica* is a variety which grows more vigorously than the above species. Particularly valuable are the large-flowered types produced by Kordes; they bear poetic names such as Frühlingsgold and Frühlingsmorgen.

ROSA WILLMOTTIAE
64

Shrub rose

Native to Europe and Asia. Tall-growing (over 6 ft) with long, arching branches and lovely small violet-pink blooms, the whole encircled in light fern-like foliage. A most graceful plant whose beauty must not be stifled among coarse flowering shrubs or evergreens. However, it is not always completely hardy and may be cut back a little by frost.

ROSE GAUJARD
45

Hybrid tea

Gaujard 1958

[Peace x a seedling from Opera]

Dark pink, tinted yellowish-white towards the centre of the flower, with silvery-white reverse. Beautiful, tightly packed flowers with a strong scent. Very vigorous growth and handsome, glossy, dark green leaves. Below hip height (30 in).

ROYAL SCARLET HYBRID
58

Climber

Chaplin 1926

Resembles Paul's Scarlet Climber, but the colour is a deeper and more vivid dark red. Very large, semi-double flowers in large clusters. Moderate growth with stems up to 6–9 ft. Both these climbers are difficult from the viewpoint of colour, when used in large numbers or when planted against a red brick wall.

RUMBA
45

Floribunda

S. Poulsen 1959

[Masquerade x (Poulsen's Bedder x Floradora)] Small, shapely flowers in large trusses. The buds are yellow at first but the colour changes to scarlet when the blooms are fully open. A characteristic type which should be used with a little care. Tight, compact growth up to about knee height (23 in).

SANDERS WHITE
58

Climber

Sanders & Sons 1912

Small, full, fragrant flowers in large, compact trusses. Long, slender, green stems up to 9–12 ft long. It will flower profusely if the old shoots are removed immediately after flowering.

SARABANDE
46

Floribunda

Meilland 1957

[Cocorico x Moulin Rouge]

Glowing orange-red, loosely packed to single flowers in large, diffuse trusses. Flowers profusely over a long period. Moderate, compact, growth to 25–30 in.

SORAYA
48

Hybrid tea

Meilland 1956

[(Peace x Independence) x Grand'mère Jenny] Buds orange-red changing to dark orange-pink when the blooms are fully open. Large, well-shaped flowers with a faint scent. Handsome, glossy reddish foliage and vigorous growth to about knee height (27 in).

SPARRIESHOOP
62

Shrub rose

W. Kordes 1953

[(Baby Château x Elsa Poulsen) x Magnifica] Large, pure pink, single or semi-double flowers in large trusses. Characteristic scent and vigorous, stiff, upright growth to about breast height.

SPARTAN
48

Floribunda, hybrid tea-type

Boerner, Jackson & Perkins 1955
[Geranium Red x Fashion]
Very large, tightly packed, orange-red flowers; almost as shapely as in the hybrid tea roses. The colour persists and the flower is very fragrant. Handsome, glossy, dark green foliage and very strong growth to about hip height (29–40 in).

SPEK'S YELLOW (GOLDEN SCEPTRE)   46
Hybrid tea
Verschuren 1947
[Golden Rapture x a seedling]
Bright yellow, shapely, scented flowers in clusters on long stiff stems. Flowers over a long period. Above knee height (27–31 in).

STELLA POLARIS   63
Shrub rose
Jenson 1890
This variety originates from *R. rugosa*, the Japanese Rose. It has large, single white flowers and apple-shaped hips which are larger than those of the parent species. Stiff growth reaching to about hip height, with underground runners; it is particularly suitable for covering slopes. Tolerates poor, loose soil and windy conditions. *R. rugosa*, the parent species of this rose and of the variety Fru Dagmar Hastrup, grows up to hip height and is particularly suitable for coastal areas as it tolerates sea-fog and salt spray.

SUNDANCE   47
S. Poulsen 1954
[Poulsen's Supreme seedling x Eugene Fürst]
Pink with pale-orange shading. Loosely packed flowers in clusters, with a faint scent. Handsome, fresh green foliage and erect, bushy growth to above knee height (27 in).

SUPER STAR   48
Hybrid tea
Tantau 1960
[(Seedling x Peace) x (Seedling x Alpine Glow)]
The pure vermilion colour is retained right from the bud until petal fall. The shapely flowers are double and have a pleasant scent. They are carried singly or a few together on very long, stiff stems and are therefore particularly suitable for

cutting. About hip height (35–40 in). This very healthy plant is certainly one of the best new rose varieties.

SUSPENSE   47
Hybrid tea
Meilland 1960
Beautiful bright red with yellow edges to the petals. Large, double blooms and flowers profusely. Robust, healthy growth to above knee height (27 in).

SUTTER'S GOLD   47
Hybrid tea
Swim 1950
[Charlotte Armstrong x Signora]
Very beautiful warm golden-yellow with bronze-red shading and veins. Large, slender, double flowers with an unusually fine, strong scent. Robust growth with handsome, glossy, dark green leaves. Above knee height (29 in).

TALISMAN   49
Hybrid tea
Montgomery 1929
[Ophelia x Souvenir de Claudius Pernet]
Warm coppery-yellow with orange-red veining and shading on the petals. The slender and elegant flowers are quite characteristic, particularly when half-expanded. Tall, robust growth with handsome foliage. Above knee height (27 in).

TAUSENDSCHÖN   58
Climber
Schmidt 1906
This seedling from Crimson Rambler has medium-sized, rose-pink, double flowers in large clusters. Slightly fragrant. Green branches, almost thornless, and strong growth with shoots up to 9–12 ft long.

TAWNY GOLD   49
Hybrid tea
M. Leenders 1951
[Vanessa x Bürgermeister van Oppen]
Beautifully shaped flowers of a characteristic matt golden-yellow colour and remarkably fragrant. Tall growth, 27–31 in, with good foliage,

but not always hardy in the open. An excellent rose for forcing.

TEXAS CENTENNIAL   49

Hybrid tea

Watkins 1935

[Sport from President Herbert Hoover]

Bright red with orange-yellow shading, elegantly shaped with a pleasant scent. Resembles President Herbert Hoover in all respects, except that the growth is lower and more bushy. Above knee height (27 in).

TIFFANY   51

Hybrid tea

R. V. Lindquist 1954

[Charlotte Armstrong x Girona]

Golden-yellow becoming deeper towards the centre; the edges of the petals are shaded salmon-pink. Fragrant, large double flowers. Glossy, dark green leaves and vigorous growth to above knee height (27–31 in).

TIVOLI   51

Floribunda

S. Poulsen 1955

[Poulsen's Supreme x (Souvenir de Claudius Denoyel x Hvissingerose)]

Pure pink with a yellowish tint towards the centre of the flower. Fragrant. Profuse flowering, vigorous growth and handsome glossy foliage. Above knee height (27–31 in).

TONI LANDER   50

Floribunda

S. Poulsen 1959

[Independence x Circus]

Bright orange-red slightly fragrant. Double flowers in loose clusters. Vigorous bushy growth to about knee height (23–29 in).

TZIGANE   50

Hybrid tea

Meilland 1951

[Peace x J. B. Meilland]

Large double flowers. Petals scarlet inside, shiny pale-yellow outside. Fragrant. Glossy dark green to reddish foliage; moderately vigorous (23 in).

ULRICH BRUNNER   53

Hybrid perpetual

A. Levet 1881

[Sport from Paul Neyron]

Flowers dark red changing to a bluish tone when fully open. Strongly scented. Very robust growth to about hip height (3 ft).

VEILCHENBLAU   58

Climbing polyantha

Schmidt 1909

[Crimson Rambler seedling]

Numerous small violet-blue, fragrant flowers in very large clusters. Only flowers once in the middle of the summer. Almost thornless, vigorous growth with stems up to 9–12 ft. Thrives on shaded walls and the colour is then more beautiful than when grown in bright sunlight, where the flowers quickly fade. The colour is difficult to mix with other roses, but it looks well with the pale yellow varieties. It is perhaps best grown with white climbing roses, and should never be put against a red wall.

VIRGO   52

Hybrid tea

Mallerin 1947

[Blanche Mallerin x Neige Parfum]

Slender, shapely, pure white flowers on long, stiff stems, and therefore very suitable for cutting. Slightly fragrant. Moderate growth (23 in), and good, glossy foliage.

WHITE DOROTHY   55

Climber

B. R. Cant 1908

A beautiful, white sport of the ordinary Dorothy Perkins (see p. 36 for description of the latter).

WILHELM HANSMANN   58

Climber

W. Kordes 1955

[(Baby Chateau x Else Poulsen) x *R. Kordesii*]

Very shapely, dark red double flowers in loose clusters. Flowers profusely from July to autumn. Healthy foliage and robust bushy growth with stems up to 6–9 ft long.

YVONNE RABIER   53

Floribunda

Turbat 1910
[*R. wichuraiana* x polyantha]
Pure white with a faint yellowish tint in the centre. Medium-sized, fragrant double flowers in large trusses. Compact, bushy growth with very handsome, glossy and persistent, almost evergreen foliage. Height about 23–31 in.

ZAMBRA   *53*
Floribunda
Meilland 1961
Bright orange-yellow flushed red, semi-double flowers in small trusses. An unusually brilliant colour which should be used with care amongst other roses. Vigorous, bushy growth to about knee height (23–27 in).

The following is a description of some completely new and valuable rose varieties which have come on the market either during or after the preparation of this book, and which deserve a brief mention here.

COPENHAGEN
Climber
N. Poulsen 1964
[Seedling x Ena Harkness]
Large, very fragrant, clear dark-red flowers which are produced throughout the summer. Vigorous growth with glossy green foliage.

ELIZABETH OF GLAMIS
Floribunda
McGredy 1964
[Spartan x Highlight]
Beautifully shaped, warm golden-orange flowers with a faint scent. Medium, erect growth to about 20 in. Dark green leaves with a reddish sheen when unfolding.

FRAGRANT CLOUD (DUFTWOLKE)
Hybrid tea
Math. Tantau 1963
[Seedling x Prima Ballerina]
A very large-flowered, dark coral-red floribunda rose. According to the breeder, it has an intoxicating and enchanting scent – hence its name. Healthy and vigorous growth with handsome foliage.

LIBERTY BELL
Hybrid tea
R. Kordes 1963
This variety, which is known as the world's largest rose, has unusually large flowers. The underside of the petals is silvery-pink, the inside and the curved outward edges are bright cinnabar-red. Vigorous growth and glossy, dark green foliage.

ORANGEADE
Floribunda

McGredy 1959
[Orange Sweetheart x Independence]
Without doubt the most brilliant orange-red colour among the floribundas. The semi-double flowers are carried in large trusses. Broad, compact growth. Height 23 in.

PASCALI
Hybrid tea
Louis Lens 1963
[Queen Elizabeth x White Butterfly]
Very elegant, soft white flowers which open very slowly. Handsome, glossy, dark green foliage which is resistant to disease and rain. Robust, tall, bushy growth. Very suitable for greenhouse cultivation.

POLKA
Floribunda *Meilland 1960*
[Moulin Rouge x Fashion]
Medium-sized, well-shaped, claret-rose, double flowers on stiff stems. Moderate growth and healthy foliage.

UNCLE WALTER
Hybrid tea *McGredy 1963*
[Brilliant x Heidelberg]
Shapely, brilliant red double flowers on unusually long stiff stems. Very tall, robust growth up to almost 6 ft, with healthy, dark green foliage.

VIENNA CHARM
Hybrid tea *W. Kordes 1963*
Large, double flowers of an exceptionally fine coppery-orange colour, which becomes somewhat more intense as the flowers open. Pleasant, strong scent. Handsome foliage and robust growth with stiff stems.

ROSE

CULTIVATION

How a new rose is created

It is not difficult to create a new rose but to create a good new rose is quite another matter. Following on from "The Cultural History of the Rose", we can now discuss in more detail the points which are important in the improvement of roses.

The genus, *Rosa*, contains about 120 species of which only eight play an important role in the innumerable rose varieties of today. From the start of the history of rose cultivation until the nineteenth century, four species were concerned: *R. gallica L., R. moschata Herrm., R. phoenicea* Boris and *R. canina L.* In the course of years crossings between these four species gave, as well as mutations, the following:

R. phoenicea x *R. gallica* = *R. damascena* (Summer Damask).

R. gallica x *R. moschata* = *R. bifera* (Autumn Damask).

R. canina x *R. gallica* = *R. alba.*

The Cottage Rose (x *R. centifolia*) probably contains all four species. The development of the centifolia roses which was undertaken by Dutch breeders reached its climax at the beginning of the eighteenth century. Mutations occurred several times and produced forms of the moss roses.

THE OLD CULTIVATED ROSES

The next big step forward in the development of the rose took place in the years around 1800. Four old cultivated varieties were introduced to Europe from the East, all of which were derived from *R. chinensis* and *R. gigantea*, and once the French, Dutch and English gardeners of this period had begun to work with intentional hybridisation, it was not long before completely new types saw the light of day.

Slater's Crimson China came to England and from there reached the United States where it was hybridised with *gallica* and Damask varieties. In the course of some decades a new group, known as

the Portland roses, was developed, and this led to the Rose du Roi, a much valued rose of the period. Portland roses are no longer grown but from this group came the Bourbon roses on the one hand and on the other the hybrid perpetual roses, of which General Jacqueminot is still known and valued by rose lovers.

Parson's Pink China made a couple of small digressions before it really made itself known. On the small island of Bourbon (now Réunion) off the east coast of Africa, they used to plant roses between the fields. For this they used the autumn-flowering Damask Rose (*R. bifera*) and Parson's Pink China. These two hybridised and in 1817, a French botanist found the offspring of this mating and immediately sent it home to France. There the rose breeders used this hybrid as a basis from which they developed a new group known as the Bourbon roses. Among the best known and most regularly cultivated of these are Coupe d'Hébé, Louise Odier and Zéphirine Drouhin.

Portland and Bourbon roses were crossed to give the hybrid perpetual group (see below).

In South Carolina a Mr Philip Noisette acquired a hybrid between Parson's Pink China and *R. moschata* which had been produced by Champneys in 1802. Further hybridisation produced the first Noisette roses, which were low-growing and double, and they flowered throughout the year. Mr Noisette sent plants to his brother in Paris and soon afterwards the Noisette roses became very popular in France. Up to 1830, the Noisette group made great progress in respect of growth, profusion of flowering and so on, but the range of flower colours was still restricted to violet-red and pink tones. It was at this time that the third type of old cultivated rose from the East came into the picture.

Park's Yellow Tea-scented China (introduced in 1824) was the first truly improved yellow rose seen in the West and by crossing with Noisette

The rose, La France. Illustration from The Floral Magazine, *1868.*

roses it not only produced low-growing, yellow, Noisette roses but also the yellow, climbing tea roses. Most rose lovers will know Gloire de Dijon and Maréchal Niel which became the two most famous varieties among the tea roses. However, like most other tea roses Maréchal Niel is not hardy enough to thrive in the open except in very warm climates.

Hume's Blush Tea-scented China (1809) also played a major role in the hybridisation work of the early nineteenth century; when crossed with the Noisettes it provided the basis for the clear, pale-pink tea roses. When again crossed with Noisettes these gave a long series of varieties in the period between 1840 and 1900.

THE NEWER CULTIVATED ROSES
One of the critical events in the breeding of modern roses occurred in 1867 when Guillot Fils of Lyons in France launched the first hybrid tea rose which was named La France. This variety was therefore the forerunner of the group which is so popular today. During the years preceding the Second World War, La France was grown continuously in many nurseries.

R. foetida Herrmann (*R. lutea Miller*) came into the picture at the end of the nineteenth century; it was brought to Europe from Persia. Although it had been in cultivation for a thousand years, it had not previously contributed by hybridisation to any of the new varieties. The reason for this was that both the pollen and ovules of *R. foetida* and of the mutation *R. foetida bicolor* (yellow and red) were almost 100% sterile. As many of the cultivated garden roses were also more or less sterile, it is understandable that it needed a great deal of patient work to break through this barrier. This was done by the French nursery firm of Pernet-Ducher in Lyons. From 1883 to 1888, they made thousands of crossings between *R. foetida* and various hybrid perpetual roses – the former providing pollen for the latter. All these crossings were unsuccessful except one, which was carried out with the variety Antoine Ducher. The seeds produced two plants of which one had 100% maternal characters while the other had a decided stamp of *R. lutea*. Pernet-Ducher carried out further hybridisation with this form and in 1900 the first Pernetiana rose was sold under the name Soleil d'Or. From then until now the Pernetiana group has undergone considerable development. All the first Pernetiana roses were susceptible to black spot but this was partly eliminated by hybridisation. We must thank Pernet-Ducher for many of the brilliant yellow and orange colours which characterise many of our modern roses.

Before closing this section on the hybrid tea roses, we must not forget to mention Ophelia, the most famous of all the hybrid teas which was raised by W. Paul in England in 1912. A number of the hybrid teas we grow today have Ophelia in their ancestry. All rose growers will be familiar not only with this variety but also with Mme. Caroline Testout, Mme. Butterfly, Crimson Glory and Talisman.

At the present time the hybrid tea group contains over 50% of cultivated garden roses.

POLYANTHA ROSES
The polyantha group (from the Greek: *poly*, many

and *anthos*, a flower) is divided nowadays into low-growing polyanthas and hybrid polyanthas, or floribundas. We owe low-growing polyantha roses, which are the first stage in the development of the whole group, to the introduction of *R. multiflora* into Europe. In 1860 seeds from this wild species were sent to Lyons, where they were sown and produced, among other things, some plants with double blooms which retained the climbing characteristic of *R. multiflora*, flowering only once. Guillot Fils crossed these double-flowered climbers with Dwarf Pink China and produced the first low-growing polyantha roses in 1875. Dwarf Pink China was originally brought from Mauritius to England in 1805 and was distributed in nurseries around Lyons. Two varieties from this cross, Pâquerette (1875) and Mignonette (1881), became the ancestral stock for nearly all the low-growing polyantha roses. Orléans Rose, an offspring of Mme. Norbert Levavasseur, is the ancestor of a considerable number of the Poulsen roses; it was derived from Gloire des Polyanthes, one of the best-known polyanthas of the period.

The appearance of the low-growing polyantha roses gave a renewed impetus to the garden roses. Although most of them had small flowers and were scentless, they were very popular on account of their hardiness and the profusion of their flowers. Only a few varieties from this group have survived, among them Ellen Poulsen (Dines Poulsen 1912).

The next major step forward in the development of garden roses came in 1912 when D. T. Poulsen launched Cardinal's Hat. The parents were Mme. Norbert Levavasseur and Richmond (a scarlet hybrid tea rose). The intention behind this cross was to combine the hardiness and profusion of flowers of the polyantha rose with the form and colour of the hybrid tea. Cardinal's Hat is still grown today, but only on account of its hardiness and resistance to disease; from the colour aspect, it cannot compare with the modern hybrid polyanthas. In 1924, Else and Kirsten Poulsen came into being, both progeny of Orléans Rose crossed with Red Star (a red hybrid tea). A few years later (1930) came D. T. Poulsen (Orléans Rose x Vesuvius (red hybrid tea)) and in 1933

The rose, Maréchal Niel. Illustration from The Floral Magazine *1863.*

Karen Poulsen (Kirsten Poulsen x Vesuvius). These roses all became widely distributed throughout the world and attained great popularity. Furthermore they inspired other rose breeders and the hybrid polyantha group has undergone considerable development, even approaching the hybrid teas in popularity.

In the years following the last war hybrid polyanthas or floribundas have developed enormously.

In addition to Dr Svend Poulsen, this work has been particularly associated with the names of W. Kordes and Mathias Tantau from Germany and of Eugene Boerner of the great American firm, Jackson and Perkins. Completely new colours have appeared and the colours of hybrid polyanthas will soon span almost the whole spectrum. However, a pure blue rose has not yet been produced and it is doubtful whether this will ever happen, because the pigment, delphinidin, which must be present to produce a true blue, is not found in any of the roses. The bluish tones seen in varieties such as Intermezzo and Prelude are due to another pigment, anthocyanin, which is also found in beetroot. To be completely blue, anthocyanin must have a pH of exactly 7. A small deviation to one side or the other immediately causes a change to either reddish or violet-red.

CLIMBERS AND RAMBLERS

Naturally the climbing roses have also undergone development during the course of time, but it has been nothing like so revolutionary as in the hybrid teas and hybrid polyanthas. It has already been mentioned that the yellow climbing tea roses, such as Maréchal Niel and others, were developed on the Noisette roses, but these were not very hardy. Up to the end of the nineteenth century these types and also some climbing varieties of hybrid teas were being grown.

An attempt at improving the climbing roses was made in England by Thomas Rivers, Bennett and others at the beginning of the twentieth century. They used the Ayrshire Rose, *R. arvensis*, which grows wild in Britain and elsewhere as one component. A smallish number of climbing Ayrshire hybrids appeared in the succeeding years, but they never became very widely distributed.

A group of shrub roses should also be mentioned here, namely the Pemberton hybrids (or hybrid musks). These originate from *R. moschata* on one side and are also closely related to the climbing Noisette roses. Most of the varieties were introduced after the first World War and in the thirties, and many of them were given mythological names such as Clytemnestra, Danae and so on. They were tried out in Denmark but although many of the varieties were quite charming, they were insufficiently hardy and their cultivation ceased. During recent years W. Kordes has done more work with this group. One of the results is Iceberg, a very popular modern variety. Even though Iceberg does not have long shoots the growth shows characteristics of *R. moschata*, being robust and vigorous; moreover, it is not susceptible to frost.

Cultivated forms of Asiatic species were often brought to Europe many years before the original species itself was seen. This happened in the case of *R. multiflora* which did not arrive in Europe until 1862, whereas a cultivated form, *R. multiflora carnea* (probably a hybrid between *R. chinensis* and *R. multiflora cathayensis*), had already reached England in 1804 via the East India Company. In the succeeding years this multiflora variety spread throughout Europe and by hybridisation with other varieties produced the first multiflora ramblers. None of these early types is grown nowadays, but the blood lives on in some of the modern climbing roses.

In 1878, R. Smith, an engineer who was a professor in Tokyo University, found Crimson Rambler in a garden in Tokyo. This discovery provided rich possibilities for improving the multiflora ramblers still further. Seen in relation to the conditions at that period, this variety was unusually beautiful, with an abundance of bright red double flowers in large clusters. It was sent to England where it became known as The Engineer's Rose, a name which was later altered (about 1893) to Crimson Rambler. Although this variety is rarely cultivated now most rose growers know of Crimson Rambler, the name given to this type of rambler rose. The best known progeny of Crimson Rambler is Tausendschön (Schmidt 1906) which is still grown in some nurseries.

Besides having given blood to the multiflora ramblers, the species itself – or forms of it – is used as a rose stock. Every year, millions of plants of *R. multiflora* are planted in all parts of the world, but more will be said of this later on.

The Prairie Rose, *R. setigera* (Michaux), a native of America, has also played a part in the development of the climbing roses. The best known is probably the delightful yellow Doubloons which does not flower very profusely and is sometimes cut back by frost. Work is still going on with *setigera* blood, and the very popular hybrid, Goldilocks, is one of the progeny. Quite a number of climbing *setigera* hybrids are still grown in the U.S.A.

The next step was the discovery of *R. wichuraiana*

R. moschata alba. *Woodcut from* Neu vollkommen Kräuterbuch, *1687, by D. Jacobus Theodorus Tabernae-montanus.*

(Crepin) on a river bank in Japan in 1861 by Dr Max E. Wichura. The first plants were sent to Germany but they all died, and it was not until 1880 that *R. wichuraiana* was grown successfully in the Botanic Gardens in Munich and Brussels. By 1890, the species had spread to various nurseries. It is to *R. wichuraiana* that we owe such lovely ramblers as American Pillar (van Fleet 1902), Dorothy Perkins (Jackson and Perkins 1901), Dr W. van Fleet (van Fleet 1910) and also Paul's Scarlet Climber (Paul 1916) and Blaze (Kallay 1932).

Before leaving the climbing roses, two contemporary rose growers must be mentioned, namely: W. Kordes of Germany and Walter D. Brownell of the U.S.A. Both are working on the development of climbing roses – Brownell using Dr W. van Fleet as basic material and Kordes a completely new species, *R. Kordesii.*

The best of Brownell's newer roses is undoubtedly Elegance (1937) which produces the most lovely double yellow roses on long stems.

The whole subject of the development of the climbing roses warrants greater detail than space permits. *R. Kordesii*, however, must be discussed more fully. In 1919 Bowditch launched a hardy rose called Max Graf. This was produced by hybridising *R. wichuraiana* and *R. rugosa*, both of which are diploids with a chromosome count of $2N = 14$. Max Graf was also diploid but completely sterile. For many years Kordes tried to hybridise with Max Graf, but without success. Then in the thirties one of nature's miracles happened – one of the flowers on Max Graf set seed without cross-fertilisation, and two of these germinated. One of them died but the other continued to grow and produced a very fertile, hardy, perpetual flowering plant. Cytological investigation showed that this plant had a double dose of chromosomes: $2N = 28$. The plant was a tetraploid and it was recognised as an amphidiploid species. Using *R. Kordesii* as a starting point, in recent years Kordes has bred various new and attractive climbing roses, which are hardy and perpetual flowering. The following three varieties in this group will undoubtedly have a great future: Wilhelm Hansmann (1955), Zweibrücken (1955) and Parkdirektor Riggers (1957).

THE DEVELOPMENT OF BUSH OR SHRUB ROSES

In the foregoing section we have seen that up to the 1800's the majority of roses were bushy and that most of them were descended from *R. gallica*, *R. moschata* and *R. damascena*. About 1800, and subsequent to the arrival of *R. chinensis* and *R. gigantea*, interest began to centre on rearing low-growing roses.

At about this time and up to the middle of the nineteenth century a completely new group was developed in Britain. Using the Burnet Rose (*R.*

spinosissima) which grows wild over most of Europe, R. Brown of Perth in Scotland in 1793 began development work which eventually yielded a list of nearly 300 varieties. These roses never became really popular on the continent, for they were susceptible to rust. A single variety, Stanwell Perpetual (1838), may however be mentioned. It was extensively cultivated up to the middle of the 1930's.

After many years of neglect it seems that the *spinosissima* group has recently regained popularity, and once again W. Kordes has carried out the pioneer work by developing an improved and more robust type of *spinosissima* hybrid. A number of good bush roses have already been produced of which the following may be mentioned: Frühlingsgold (1937), Frühlingsmorgen (1941) and Frühlingsduft (1949).

The Sweet Briar, *R. eglanteria* L. has also contributed blood to several bush roses, of which some varieties, such as Amy Robsart, Lucy Bertram and Anne of Geierstein are still cultivated. These varieties and many others were raised by Lord Penzance in the years 1890–1895.

After an interval of several years, W. Kordes again took up the eglanteria group, using *R. eglanteria magnifica* (Hesse 1918) as the male parent and various hybrid teas or hybrid polyanthas as the female parent; from these Kordes has produced a whole series of new varieties – both low- and tall-growing – which are all robust and have healthy, vigorous foliage.

Thus Chinatown (Niels Poulsen 1960) has Sweet Briar blood in its veins, the male parent being Claire Grammersdorf (W. Kordes) which was an (*eglanteria* seedling x Peace) x an *eglanteria* seedling, while the female parent was Columbine (S. Poulsen 1956) = Danish Gold x Frensham. The coming years will doubtless bring good new roses with Sweet Briar blood.

The Japanese Rose, *R. rugosa* Thunberg, has also contributed a great deal to the development of shrub roses. We have already seen how *R. Kordesii* is descended from *R. rugosa* on the maternal side. The number of definite *rugosa* hybrids is very restricted, but as some of them are used extensively in home gardens in Denmark as well as in Norway and Sweden, they ought to be mentioned here: Fru Dagmar Hastrup (Hastrup), Signe Relander (Dines Poulsen 1928), Blanc Double de Coubert (Cochet-Cochet 1892) and F. J. Grootendorst (De Goey 1918). The original *R. rugosa* is known to most gardeners and it has been planted by the thousand in coastal areas. It was formerly very popular as an underplanting for garden roses, but this use has almost ceased on account of its tendency to produce suckers. It is still used extensively for standards.

Several other species have helped to beautify our gardens and many of these have also been under the scrutiny of the rose-breeder. It would be too much to go into them in any detail as there is very little knowledge of these species and hybrids in Britain. However, one thing stands out clearly – there are still possibilities of producing completely new types of roses. Some 7–8 species have contributed significantly to modern roses, but there are more than a hundred other possibilities, which are only waiting to be used. Many have been tried and have been rejected at the first-generation stage, but several generations may be necessary before a result is obtained.

During the last 30 years, rose-breeding has become more and more intensive. A growing knowledge of heredity, together with increased competition and protective laws concerning the rights of breeders have all made rose-breeding into an industry. Competition takes place in a friendly atmosphere, everyone knows everyone else and meets on an equal footing to discuss, compete and appraise. Idealism is combined with business; in short, rose-growing has become a glorious form of sport.

We undoubtedly owe a deep debt of gratitude to pioneers such as Guillot Fils, Pernet-Ducher, Mallerin, McGredy, Dickson, Bentley, Paul, Kordes, Tantau, Meilland, Poulsen and many others for the inspiration which has made it possible to continue improving the most beautiful of all flowers – the rose.

THE CREATION OF A NEW ROSE

It should be of interest both to the amateur and to the nurseryman to learn how a new rose is created. Let us now look at what the rose-breeder does.

To produce a new rose it is only necessary to have ripe seed from the varieties to be hybridised. But to produce a good new rose requires greenhouses, patience, "know how" and, not least, an element of luck. If a man has all these four attributes, he may have a chance of producing something good.

In our climate, the rose hip will only ripen if the conditions are particularly favourable. Therefore a greenhouse, preferably heated, is an absolute necessity. The greenhouse can be large or small, but it must be light and well ventilated. To facilitate the fight against mildew, it is an advantage to have electricity to which a sulphur vaporiser can be connected. The varieties which are to be crossed, whether male or female parents, are planted in fresh, well-manured soil. The choice of varieties is naturally difficult, and here one must rely principally on experience. Attention must be paid to several criteria, such as flower colour, flower form, number and quality of petals, scent, the tendency to shed the petals after flowering, the capacity to produce flowers, the colour and quality of the leaves, resistance to rust, mildew and black spot, hardiness, ability to grow on after budding and to produce robust plants in the nursery.

All this and a great deal more can indeed create sufficient problems. The knowledgeable rose breeder knows from experience that certain varieties give offspring with vigorous foliage and good resistance; it is his job, therefore, to add good blooms with stiff stems to such plants – blooms with colour and scent.

It may take several generations, with repeated selection and back-crossing before the desired result is even in sight. The rose-breeder crosses brother and sister or aunt and nephew to get a result and often, indeed only too frequently, the result is nil. Out of 3000 crossings one may perhaps obtain 20,000 seedlings and with good luck one ends up with two or three which are found worthy of inclusion in the list of varieties.

HYBRIDISATION

The technique of crossing is not in itself very difficult. When the flowers chosen as the female parents are in the last bud stage, that is just before they open out, the male organs or stamens are removed; this is the process of emasculation. This operation must be done very carefully, because the presence of even a very little pollen can cause complete or partial self-fertilisation, and this is certainly not the intention. Some varieties have to be emasculated at an early bud stage, because their stamens elongate before the flower has opened. The simplest method of carrying out emasculation is first to remove the petals with the fingers and then to cut out the stamens with a very sharp knife, without damaging the stigma (the female organ). To avoid cross-pollination by insects a plastic bag is then placed over the emasculated flower. One must be prepared to emasculate from morning to evening, for the flowers will not wait until the breeder has time, and in strong

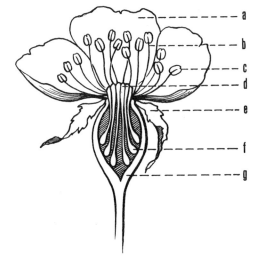

Section through a rose flower. a. petal, b. filament of stamen, c. anther, d. stigma, e. sepal, f. ovule, g. fruit.

Hybridisation technique. 1. the fully developed rose – the female parent. 2. the petals are carefully removed; in some rose varieties the emasculation has to be done as early as the bud stage. 3. the denuded flower is now ready for the actual process of emasculation itself. 4. in emasculation the male sexual organs, or stamens, have to be removed. This operation is done with a sharp knife and

sunlight it is not many hours before a bud has opened out and self-pollination has taken place.

Going through the list of proposed crossings, prepared in the course of the winter, the breeder selects the special male parent he wishes to use. Pollen from this parent can be collected the day before – or some days before – and kept very dry in a glass reagent dish, or it can be taken directly from the flower. Using a small, fine, completely dry camel-hair brush, pure pollen is transferred to the stigma, a plastic bag is placed over the whole and the female or seed parent is labelled with the male parent's name or with a code number. It is obvious that a clean paintbrush must be used when collecting pollen from a different male parent. The brushes are washed in alcohol after use. A few days after pollination has taken place, the sepals are removed with a sharp knife, partly to prevent them taking too much strength from the hip and partly to remove a possible site for fungus.

If pollination has been successful, the pollen tubes will have grown down through the stigma to the ovules, and the fruits will start to swell in the course of the next few weeks, and ripen in 6–7 months. Unsuccessful pollination may be due to several causes, such as sterility in the male or female parent, or to intersterility between these two individuals. It may also be caused by the attack of fungi which destroy the pollen tubes. Such fungal attacks frequently occur when the air in the greenhouse is too humid.

In the course of the summer and the first months of autumn the fruits should develop into large, red or orange-red hips. It frequently happens that the seeds emerge and sit in a ring above the hip. The menace of fungal attack is present throughout this period, so the greenhouse must be kept as clean as possible; all dead branches, flowers and leaves must be removed as well as any hips that show signs of fungus. It will also be necessary to dip or spray all the hips one or more times with Orthocide or a copper preparation. To prevent the plants with hips from growing too vigorously, watering is reduced to a minimum in August and September. The hips will not ripen properly if the plants receive too much water during the autumn months.

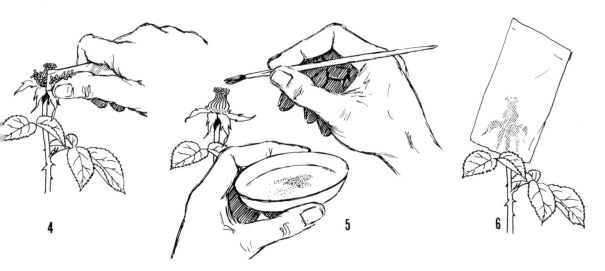

care must be taken not to damage the female sexual organs, or stigma. 5. a soft, clean paintbrush is used for the actual pollination. The pollen of the male parent is collected beforehand in a shallow dish. 6. to prevent pollination from outside – by insects – it is advisable to slip a plastic bag over the pollinated flower.

Harvesting of the ripe hips begins in November. The seeds from each cross are kept separate, given a code number and put in a plastic bag with damp vermiculite or sphagnum moss. To obtain good germination the seeds must not be allowed to dry out. Crosses involving hybrid tea roses are kept separately from hybrid polyanthas, because the former usually germinate very slowly, sometimes not until a year after they are sown.

CULTIVATION AND SELECTION

About the middle of February the seeds are sown in a bed in the greenhouse, and the first plants begin to appear 6–8 weeks later. The soil in the seed bed or at least its upper layer should preferably be sterile. The bed should have a soil depth of 12 inches, the lower 7 inches consisting of ordinary light farm soil, the upper 5 inches being a mixture of steamed soil, sphagnum and vermiculite. The seedlings must be kept growing throughout the summer by appropriate watering and the addition of fertiliser.

Although it may seem that both the crossing and the handling of the seeds sounds very com-plicated, the most difficult part has yet to come, namely the selection of the many different little rose plants. The first flowers appear 10–15 weeks after the seed is sown and this is, I suppose what fascinates the rose breeder most. He must go and examine the flowers several times every day, running through the list of crosses to check on the parents and grandparents. One is often surprised when one knows the parents and sees their progeny. There may perhaps be only a few characters in common, but on looking at their pedigree one can recognise pronounced traits inherited from the grandparents and great-grandparents. There are always surprises, for however much thought has been given to the crosses, the result is never 100% predictable.

Selection goes on throughout the summer. Several times a day the breeder has to go through the beds of seedlings and weed out any plants that can be discarded in advance. These may be plants which carry flowers with impure colours, or flowers which should be full but which have too few petals; plants with poor foliage and suscept-ibility to mildew must also be removed at the same time. Plants which show promising character-istics are marked with a stick and given a code number, which is used for this special clone until in the following year it may *perhaps* be given a name.

In August the selected rose plants have to be propagated. This takes place out in the open by budding (see page 64) and the practice is to bud from 5 to 25 plants of each variety, according to their apparent promise.

The next selection takes place in the following year. The tiny plants now have a strong rootstock and their appearance has changed quite a bit. Alongside their own seedlings most rose breeders cultivate several new, numbered varieties from other breeders to test them out. It is extremely important for a rose breeder to know what is happening in the "workshops" of other breeders; one can become mesmerised by one's own seed-lings and become blind to the fact that they are far below foreign standards.

So the second selection takes place during this summer. Fifty to two hundred of each of 25–50 of the best numbers are budded, and at the same time buds, or "eyes" (see page 64), of the very best are sent to the foreign firms which grow one's roses under licence.

Section through a ripe hip, showing the seeds.

THE FINAL RESULT

One must reject and select and often one makes mistakes, for at this stage it is possible to bypass a plant which in the coming year shows itself to be a winner.

The next selection is made in the third summer after the seedlings have flowered for the first time. In the autumn six plants of each of the best varieties are sent to the international testing grounds which are situated throughout Europe and Japan. The United States also has testing gardens – 23 of them – to which American breeders send their novelties. European firms can also participate, but only by working through an American firm. In these gardens the roses are judged over a period of two years. The test cultiva-tion ends with selection of the best roses.

The roses are then ready to be named and sent out by the nurseries into the trade channels. To find a good name which will be acceptable inter-nationally may be about as difficult as producing a new rose. No modern breeder would use a name such as Souvenir de la Princesse Amélie des Pays-Bas, which a Frenchman gave to a purplish-red hybrid perpetual rose in 1872. The name must be short and capable of being pronounced in the principal languages. Polka, Rumba and Piccadilly are excellent examples of this. After the final selection a breeder will sit down with his rose-enthusiast friends and discuss names. Sug-gestions, more or less fantastic, are criticised and evaluated and as a rule rejected, but suddenly the right name will come for the right rose.

About three years ago, Samuel McGredy of Northern Ireland christened the rose Chinatown (see colour plate 11) as the result of a conversation which, by devious routes, finished up on the Chinese quarter in San Francisco.

TRIAL GROUNDS

In the foregoing section, the international trial cultivation of new roses was mentioned briefly. This section tells where the most important rose gardens are found. All of these work on the same principle – a two-year period of trial followed by selection.

Judging roses in the Parc de Bagatelle in Paris on 19th June 1933. This was the first trial ground, where cultivation over a period of two years was a condition for participating in the annual competition. Only two gold medals were awarded, one for the best French rose, the other for the best foreign rose. As seen here this involved considerable discussion, but everything ended in amity at the traditional luncheon where the French Government were hosts.

Holland A beautiful rose garden (rosarium) was opened in 1961 at the bathing resort of Scheveningen near the Hague; this has a closed section for testing new roses. The rose garden is situated in a public park, Westbroekpark, and is well worth a visit. Over 20,000 roses have been planted and the number increases annually. Each year in July they carry out a selection after the two-year trial period. The jury consists partly of Dutch rose experts and partly of foreign rose-breeders.

Spain Parque del Retiro in Madrid is one of the most beautiful rose gardens in Europe. It has thousands of roses attractively planted in beds and over pergolas. In the evening, the garden is illuminated and music from an orchestra floats gently through the park. After the selection which takes place in June there is an official opening of the garden, led by the Papal Nuncio and the Mayor. Anyone who is in Madrid in June or July should not miss this experience.

France Europe's oldest test garden, Le Parc de Bagatelle, is beautifully situated in the Bois de Boulogne in Paris. Work began on the rose garden in 1903 and the first new roses were selected in 1907. For many years, Bagatelle was the rose breeder's Mecca, but the establishment of trial gardens in many other countries has shifted the emphasis somewhat in favour of St Albans and the Hague.

Italy The Italian International Rose Garden is situated at the Piazzale Romolo e Remo in Rome;

Budding and grafting. 1. a rose branch with "eyes" (buds). 2. the eye selected for budding. 3. the bud with bark and splint. 4. a special budding knife is used to cut the bud from the branch. 5. at a point near the level of the soil a T-shaped incision is made in the main stem of the stock, as we call the wild rose used for this purpose. 6. here the eye has been inserted into the T-slit and the flaps of bark folded together around it. 7. raffia is tied around the stem to hold the bud in the T-slit.

it is not quite so large as the garden in Paris. Roses come here from all over the world for annual gold and silver awards.

England The Royal National Rose Society's Garden at Bone Hill, St Albans, lies about an hour's train journey from London. The Royal National Rose Society is a body of rose enthusiasts which has over 100,000 members in the British Isles, and is thus the largest rose society in the world. The test cultivation finishes with judging and making awards to the best varieties. Adjoining the Trial Grounds at St Albans is a large display garden which contains a very representative collection of roses old and new. To receive a gold medal at St Albans means that almost 100,000 gardeners will get to know about it through the Royal National Rose Society's *Rose Annual*; the good news spreads very quickly.

Other foreign test gardens Among these we may mention the Swiss garden at Geneva, not far from the Lake of Geneva. Germany has a test garden at the well-known spa of Baden-Baden. Here the judging is a festive occasion carried out in association with the spa hotel. A trial garden

was established in Belgium in 1963 and the first selections took place in 1965.

Denmark Denmark's trial ground is situated in Valby Park, Copenhagen. Due to the initiative of Mr J. Bergmann, the City Gardener and of Dr Svend Poulsen, and supported by the Copenhagen City Council, a rose garden has been created which is perhaps one of the most beautiful in Europe.

About 12,000 roses are planted within a circular area of about 3¾ acres, with a diameter of 140 yards. The borders are planted with bush roses of which there are about 100 varieties, both old and new. There are about 65 varieties of polyanthas and floribundas and a similar number of hybrid teas. Some 20 varieties of climbing rose grow on a pergola. Apart from the bush roses, the idea is that the assortment of low-growing roses shall be up to date, so that only varieties grown in the nurseries find a place in the rose garden.

In a smaller, closed area by the side of the rose garden is the trial ground, which is based on the international pattern. Every year new roses are called for from breeders all over the world, and

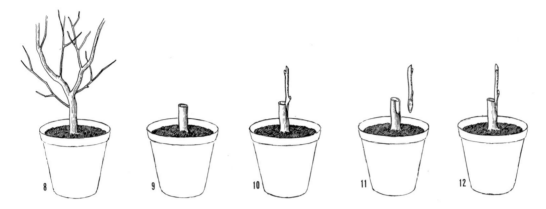

8. the stock used for grafting. 9. the stock is cut down horizontally. 10. an example of wedge-grafting. The graft is inserted in a slit cut in one side of the stock. 11. an example of rind-grafting. A vertical cut is made in the bark of the stock and the graft is cut off obliquely at its base. 12. the obliquely cut graft is placed against the stock. In both wedge-grafting and rind-grafting the stock and scion are bound together.

these are planted under standard conditions. Six plants of each low-growing variety and two each of the climbing and bush roses are asked for. The new roses sent in are regularly judged throughout two seasons of growth by a standing committee of judges, and only those which thrive under Danish conditions receive awards.

Varieties which take part in the trial cultivation are not allowed to be put up for sale until the testing is complete. In the final judging in summer 1965 about 60 new varieties competed for the highest points.

The Scandinavian rose-growing association, Nord-Rose, has taken the initiative in this trial ground, with a view to finding the most suitable new varieties for Scandinavian conditions from among the large supply of novelties which go around the rose breeders every year.

Valby Park was officially opened in July 1964. Rose experts from Britain, Ireland, Belgium, Germany and Holland and from the Scandinavian countries assisted the permanent judging committee with a final assessment that gave the following result.

Uncle Walter – an attractive large-flowered floribunda type with showy, dark red flowers

was awarded the Gold Medal of the Danish Gardeners' Association and the Gold Medal of Nord-Rose.

Elizabeth of Glamis, a scented floribunda with large full blooms, of a deep pink colour with orange-yellow shading, was awarded the Gold Medal of the Danish Nurserymen's Association and the Gold Medal of Nord-Rose.

Both varieties were raised by the well-known rose breeder, Samuel D. McGredy IV of Northern Ireland.

At the opening a public vote was taken to choose the three most popular roses in the open garden. The highest number of points was obtained by Super Star (Mathias Tantau, Germany). After this came Lilli Marlene (Reimer Kordes, Germany) and third place was taken by Toni Lander (Dr Svend Poulsen, Copenhagen).

Before leaving the subject of trial grounds some mention must be made of a rose garden in Sweden which for several years was used as a testing ground for Nord-Rose. This was established about 10 years ago in the old Danish royal castle of Backaskog Kungsgard, about 12 miles from Kristianstad, as a cooperative effort by the Swedish nurseries and Consultant Fehrlenius.

Nord-Rose came into the picture somewhat later, but they have now moved their trials to Valby Park which is more central.

HOW ROSE PLANTS ARE "MANUFACTURED"
The use of improved rose plants is on a larger scale today than at any other time. Some 100 million rose plants are sold annually in all parts of the world, and their value is hundreds of thousands of pounds. The rose is an international plant which will grow anywhere except in the extremely cold regions. In Denmark between 10 and 12 million roses are budded every year, and considerable numbers of the finished products are exported.

Under the section on raising new roses we referred to the fact that these are produced by sexual reproduction which yields seeds. This method of reproduction cannot, however, be used to obtain a clone population, that is, a stock of roses which are all absolutely identical. For this, vegetative reproduction by grafting or budding must be used.

Grafting is used principally in greenhouse cultivation where the roses are grown for cutting. The roses are grafted in January, February and March on seedlings of the Dog Rose, *R. canina*, and planted out directly from the propagation beds into the borders in the greenhouse.

Rose budding was first used in a big way in 1850 by the well-known old rose firm of Guillot Fils of Lyons. This method did not become universal in nurseries until the end of the nineteenth century.

The propagation of a rose extends over two growing seasons, from the moment the stock is obtained until the new plant is ready for sale.

The stocks are usually produced in special nurseries. The two main species used are *R. multiflora* and *R. canina*. The latter species is mostly used for varieties intended for forcing and for some hybrid teas. The Danish Research Station, Hornum has a big programme of research in hand aimed at finding the most suitable types of stock.

The stocks are planted out in the early months of spring and are regularly sprayed against pests and fungal attacks. The budding itself takes place from mid-July into September.

Using a very sharp knife the bark is cut away behind an "eye" or bud (see drawing). The splint of wood inside the bark is carefully removed and the piece of bark with the eye is pushed down into a T-shaped incision (see drawing) which has previously been made in the stock just above its roots. The piece is bound in with raffia or a rubber band, and if the operation is successful the eye will have grown in together with the stock in the course of a few weeks.

In mid-February the stock is cut back to just above the T-shaped incision, and in the course of the spring the eye from the selected rose will begin to sprout. To encourage side-shoots the scion rose is nipped above the third or fourth leaf. In the course of the summer the roses must be checked regularly and any shoots of the wild stock removed. The roses are also sprayed alternately with sulphur and copper preparations against mildew and black spot. Sometimes they get a severe attack of aphids, which are easily removed by an insecticide.

By the beginning of October the plants are ready for sale, and during the autumn the rose garden is completely dug over and the plants sorted according to quality. Those that are not sold during the autumn are placed in a refrigerated store at $\frac{1}{2}$°C (32.9°F) or heeled in for use in the spring sale. Many firms use the winter months to pack the rose plants in plastic bags, thus speeding up the spring dispatch. With a cool store, which many nurseries now have, it is possible to extend the planting time until far into the summer.

It therefore takes two years from the time the stocks arrive in the nursery until the roses go out as merchandise. There are many hazards on the way, such as breakage by wind, or mechanical injury during spraying and cleansing, and frost damage is not uncommon. It is even worse when the weather conditions are bad during the budding period (July–September); this happened for example in 1963 when the results in many

Danish nurseries were far below the average. Normally Danish nurseries reckon on about 65–70% of top quality plants, but after the 1963 budding this figure fell to 25–30% in many places.

From all this it will be seen that a rose plant has to pass through many hands before it is planted by the owner of a garden. In spite of the big rise in costs of production during recent years, Denmark continues to be one of the countries where rose prices are lowest – thanks to rationalisation and specialisation.

In Britain rose-breeders can now protect their new varieties under the provisions of the Plant Varieties and Seeds Act, 1964. This fulfilled a long-standing need, and it is to be hoped that it will stimulate both amateurs and professionals in the production of new and better roses.

Planting, pruning and general care of roses

Whether one intends to make a special rose garden or merely to plant a few beds in the lawn, a thorough preparation of the soil beforehand is essential to successful cultivation. It should be remembered that one has to produce good conditions not just for a few years, but for 15–20 years of good, vigorous growth for the varieties selected.

If the initial preparation of the soil is skimped, neither artificial manure nor other media for improving the soil will help later on.

THE SOIL

It is sometimes said that good, vigorous roses can be grown in any kind of soil, but this is an over-statement. It would be better to say that fairly good roses can be grown in any soil provided it has been improved to a greater or lesser extent.

Pure sandy soil or black, cold and wet bog-earth will however almost inevitably bring disappointing results in spite of the most energetic efforts and considerable expense; with conditions of this type it is better not to attempt to grow roses.

On the other hand, loams with a large content of sand or very stiff, clayey soil can be made into good rose soils if their unsuitable characteristics are changed. Light sandy soil requires the addition of leafmould, old manure, peat, compost or other loam-forming substances; heavy clay soil needs a proportion of sharp gravel (from a gravel-pit not from the shore) with loam-forming substances such as peat, compost, etc. It is very difficult to describe the ideal soil for roses, it needs to be seen or tested with a digging fork in the hand or examined directly by taking a handful and smelling it.

Nevertheless, let us attempt to describe the kind of soil which every gardener and rose lover should try to attain before planting his roses.

In the ideal soil the uppermost layer or top spit as it is called (about 10 inches thick) should be very rich in nutrients, that is, it should be a good loam containing the commonest plant nutrients in suitable amounts (potassium, nitrogen, phosphoric acid, micronutrients, etc.) and have a pH of 6–7. It should also have a porous, crumbly structure, that is it should crumble easily when dug with a fork or when the surface is prepared with a hand cultivator.

Information on the nutrient content and pH can be found by sending samples to the County Horticultural Department. These people will also indicate what substances should be added to the soil to make it really satisfactory for the cultivation of roses. (For further details on soil analysis and plant nutrients, see *The Soil and its Fertility*, by H. Teuscher and R. Adler (Reinhold Publishing Corporation, New York).

Under the best conditions, the second spit may be of the same good quality as the top spit, if the loam layer is about 20 inches thick or more. Usually however it will contain a certain amount of clay which will not damage the roses provided it is rendered porous and "alive".

The soil should therefore be dug over very thoroughly with a fork and a proportion of coarse gravel (e.g. 2–4 inches or more) added. Finally, if the second spit is very stiff and clayey, the bottom below it can be thoroughly loosened with a fork before layers 1 and 2 are replaced. The preparation of the soil in this way can best be understood by reference to the drawings on page 69.

It will now be clear that the primary object in preparing the soil for roses is to make it porous, to give it a kind of gritty or coarse-grained consistency so that water and air can easily penetrate the soil layers. This allows the roots of the plants to thrive and to spread out into a network which can take up water and nutrients.

This is the reason for the deep, thorough working of the soil and for the admixture of coarse gravel and peat.

The newly planted roses will mainly produce fine roots in the upper, loamy, well-worked spit

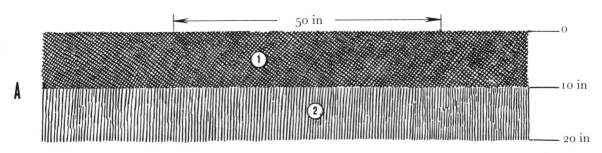

Preparation of the soil before planting garden roses is very important. A shows the soil layers before preparation: (1) the topsoil layer is about 10 inches thick. (2) the subsoil, often a sandy loam, stiff clay or sandy layer, which has to be rendered porous.

The topsoil is dug up and laid aside in a pile to the left, while the lower spit is dug up and laid to the right. The bottom (3), which is now about 20 inches below the ground level, is then loosened with a digging fork. If the bottom is stiff clay a layer of coarse gravel can be incorporated in it. The subsoil already removed (2) can also be mixed with some gravel and peat.

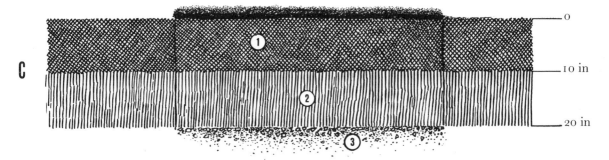

Finally the topsoil (1) is replaced, after the removal of any weed roots. If the topsoil is very clayey or poor and sandy, a layer of old manure or peat can be placed on top of it (the dark "woolly" layer in C).

and these will take up nutrients from the soil. Strong roots will grow down into the lower spit and below, and these will fetch water to the plants during dry periods in summer.

Notice that we say "fetch water", but the deep roots must never stand in water-logged soil and the level of the ground water should never be such that this can happen, either in summer or winter. If it should occur, the roses will appear sickly – and wither away completely if the conditions are not changed.

If there is any possibility of the water level being high, the soil should be drained in the area of the rose beds. Drainage is done by laying unglazed clay pipes at suitable depths so as to lead the excess water away or into a common drain; this will require professional advice.

during digging; this increases the soil's porosity and "brings it to life" by increasing the supply of oxygen.

This is the time for the soil analysis to be done, to find the pH and nutrient content. The test sample should be taken as soon as the soil has been worked and thoroughly mixed.

Once the soil analysis is available, one adds the necessary quantities of those nutrients – potassium, nitrogen, phosphate and so on – which are present in inadequate amounts. After this the soil can be lightly forked or raked with a motor harrow, and it is then ready for planting. It must be emphasised that fresh horse manure should not be mixed in with the soil either now or later on.

The soil should be thoroughly soaked if it has become dry after the deep-digging or harrowing.

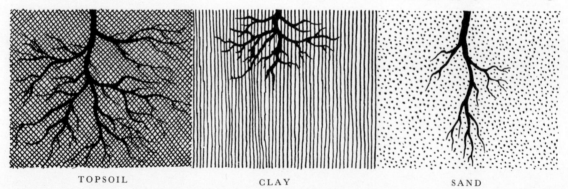

TOPSOIL   CLAY   SAND

Roses thrive best in porous soil and if this is also rich in nutrient the results will be excellent. This diagram shows clearly how important the nature of the soil is for the spread of the roots, a porous soil giving the largest network of roots and at the same time the most vigorous plants.

The sequence of jobs involved in preparing a good soil for roses is to dig and thoroughly work the soil to a depth of two spits (see p. 69).

When digging, the soil must be carefully cleansed of all kinds of perennial weeds, dandelions, thistles, quickgrass, bindweed, and so on; if it is very unclean and full of weed roots, it is a good idea to let it lie fallow over the summer, pulling up new shoots and roots as often as possible, and spraying it early in spring with a hormone solution.

Gravel and peat are also added to the soil

This must however depend on local judgment, and on the weather conditions.

THE ACTUAL PLANTING

All kinds of roses, whether large-flowered, shrub roses, climbers or floribundas can be planted from the middle of October to about the 1st of December and from the middle of March to right on into May. But this is in all cases dependent upon the weather, which in Britain varies considerably from year to year.

We may get a short period with severe black

frost at the end of October and right into November, and it may also freeze hard until far into April; in such circumstances, planting will be not only inadvisable but probably impossible.

The purchased plants must then be heeled-in in a heap of peat, loose earth or gravel.

On the other hand, the weather during these periods may be abnormally humid with so much rain that the soil even if well worked beforehand, becomes soggy and unsuitable for planting. And let us reiterate – for this is important – that a really wet soil is quite unsuitable for planting new rose plants – indeed it would be better to have a trace of frost on the surface.

The private rose-grower should have no difficulty in getting a few days in either autumn or spring in which to plant the relatively small number of plants needed in the rose garden. Experience shows that it does not matter whether the roses are planted in autumn or spring. The important thing is that the soil should be in just the right state – that is, sufficiently damp but not to such an extent that it sticks to the tools; it should crumble easily and trickle in among the plant roots.

Nowadays, of course, there are ways of prolonging the planting season. The roses are delivered packed in plastic bags with damp peat or they are kept in a state of suspension in a refrigerated store. This means that they can be planted in June, provided that they are given two thorough waterings after planting and shaded with spruce twigs or a similar screen.

We can now look a little more closely at the actual job of planting, but first it should be remembered that the plant's roots must be properly packed and dampened in the nursery before they are transported to the garden. If the roses cannot be planted immediately, they should be unpacked and heeled-in in soil, damp peat or gravel in a shady place, until planting can take place.

As already mentioned, the soil should not be too wet or stick too firmly to the spade. Begin by digging a hole for each plant, about the width

of a spade and at least a good spade's depth; it must be sufficiently deep for the roots not to be at all bent when planted.

It is useful to have two people at work on the planting. One person can then hold the plant with the roots hanging down in the hole and at such a depth that the position of the budding comes an inch or so below the surface of the soil; the other person can then fill in the loosely dug earth around the roots. While this is going on the plant should be gently shaken so that the soil penetrates between even the finest rootlets. The hole should be about three-quarters filled and the soil firmly trodden with one foot, while the plant is held in position; thus it is not pressed too deeply into the soil.

Refrigerated storage and packing in plastic bags allows roses to be planted until far on into the spring. The newly planted rose should be thoroughly watered and the parts above ground sheltered with twigs for a short time.

The newly planted rose should then be thoroughly watered a couple of times, and when the water has soaked in, the remainder of the soil can be filled in around the plant. In the case of autumn planting some extra soil is usually heaped up around the branches, or in spring planting a layer of damp peat (2 inches thick) is placed around the plant to retain the moisture.

If the roses are planted late, in June, the tops should be shaded by sticking some old spruce twigs or cut evergreen twigs around the plant, particularly on the sunny side.

PRUNING AND GENERAL CARE

A newly planted rose bush should be severely pruned in the spring. If planted in autumn the branches can be slightly shortened (by 2–4 inches) and then the full pruning can be done in spring – during the month of April – after the heaped-up earth has been scraped away.

Newly planted roses should therefore be cut back in spring; in practice, this means that only about 2–6 inches of the branches are left sticking up above ground; this applies to all groups of roses. The purpose is to promote vigorous shoot formation as close as possible to the ground and thus to begin immediately the formation of a well-branched crown on the young plant.

In pruning the first job is to cut away all very thin, half-withered or damaged branches using a pair of secateurs. Then cut off the sound, thick branches just above a firm bud, which as far as possible should face outwards or away from the centre of the bush (see drawing, p. 74). When the newly planted roses start to form fresh young shoots during the course of May, it is usually a good idea to give them a couple of thorough soakings. Scrape away a little of the earth around each plant and let the water run slowly so that it really penetrates the soil.

In May, when several of the new shoots have reached a length of 8–10 inches or more, the first small flower buds will appear, usually at the tips of the shoots. In spite of any feelings to the contrary, these shoots must be nipped off at the tips, removing

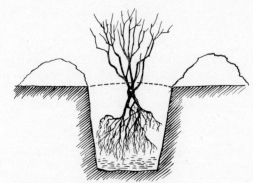

In planting, the roots should be spread so that they do not bend or stick together. The soil is distributed among the roots, while shaking the whole plant at the same time. The position where budding was carried out should be placed a little below the soil surface, and when the hole is ¾-full the soil should be firmly trodden down. The plant is then thoroughly watered and the remainder of the soil filled in. During dry periods in spring a layer of damp peat-moss should be placed around the plant; in the case of autumn-planting loose soil should be heaped up around the bush.

the outermost ¾–1 inch with the small buds – though this is only practised with maiden stems from stock budded the previous year. The purpose of this slightly brutal operation will become apparent a couple of weeks later, when numerous, small, vigorous side-shoots will appear, which will flower somewhat later. In this way we get a more branched bush and many more flowers – although admittedly about a fortnight later than normal. But in any case, we now have a stronger, more branched bush, which will fill up its space in the bed and will flower profusely in the future.

At the same time as this nipping in May, the first dose of artificial manure can be strewn around each plant. This should be done in dry weather when the plants are dry and not after rain or watering, or the artificial manure will inevitably remain hanging on the wet shoots and leaves and cause scorching.

Each rose bed can be given 2 ounces per square yard of calcium nitrate or ammonium sulphate. The plants can be carefully and gently watered after the fertiliser has been spread.

The removal of withered flowers ought not to

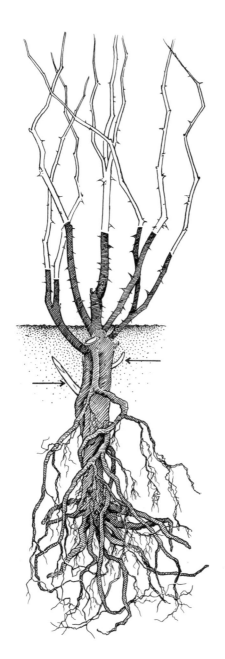

be undertaken according to a single programme but, like the annual spring pruning, should vary according to the rose group that is being dealt with (see drawings, pp. 75–77).

In floribunda roses and hybrid teas the withered blooms should be removed along with a really long stem – in the floribundas with 8–10 inches of stem and in the hybrid teas with 4–8 inches. In the large clusters of the floribundas one can however begin to remove individual withered flowers from the umbel and leave the remainder until the last blooms have withered. In the old-fashioned hybrid perpetual roses the withered flowers should be removed with only a short length of stem (2–4 inches); the same applies to the large-flowered climbers. On the other hand, in the small-flowered climbing roses the whole flower cluster can be pruned with 12–20 inches of stem and in the following year the whole shoot can be removed right down to the ground immediately after flowering.

ANNUAL PRUNING OF ROSES

A glance at the drawings on pages 75–76 will explain better than any words the annual recurrent work in the rose garden. Let us first explain briefly exactly why garden roses have to be pruned and why some have to be cut back severely whereas others only need to be thinned out every few years. In other words, why is it that garden roses, particularly hybrid teas and floribundas require annual pruning while rhododendron bushes, ornamental cherries and many other plants do not need to be pruned every year and yet flower profusely?

The newly planted rose should be pruned immediately after planting, whether this has been done in spring or autumn. The bush should be pruned right back the first time; in succeeding years pruning can be less severe, varying according to the main groups (see drawings, pp. 75–77). The budding position should be 1–2 inches below the soil surface. Any pale shoots on the root-stock should be removed with a sharp knife (see arrows). The numerous fine roots must be carefully preserved and should never be exposed to the light. Damaged or extra long, thick roots can be lightly pruned with a sharp knife.

When pruning roses it is absolutely essential to have good secateurs (see drawing, p. 79), and it is important to prune the twigs and branches properly. Dead branches should be cut off smoothly down to fresh wood or to a little below the dead wood. Fresh branches and twigs are cut off with a smooth cut as shown in (e). In (a) too much wood has been left above the bud; in (b) the cut is too close to the bud; in (c) the cut is ragged, and in (d) too oblique. Always prune down to a firm bud and never to a loose unripe bud or to one which has begun to sprout.

The explanation is simply that rose bushes form flower buds and flowers on the tips of young shoots (summer shoots), which grow out from buds on the branches during May–June; on the other hand, rhododendrons and others form new flower buds after flowering; these overwinter, and each produces a flower in June.

A rose bush is also biologically a little closer to the perennials, that is, some of the top of the plant dies back in winter because roses never manage to "ripen" their wood completely in autumn. Also a proportion of the branches will normally be killed by winter frost.

Unless pruned every spring, an ordinary garden rose will therefore end up by becoming a tight besom full of dead, half-shrivelled branches and twigs, in among which the new shoots will grow out and produce flowers. But as the years go by the whole plant will become an ugly half-withered thicket with fewer and smaller flowers.

The purpose of pruning roses is therefore first and foremost to allow light and air to reach the new shoots and later the flowers. As a general principle it can be said that the more a rose plant is pruned the more vigorous will be the shoots and the larger the flowers. On the other hand, with too little pruning the shoots will become very

numerous but few flowers will be produced. It can be shown quite clearly that each individual rose bush, including its root system, has only a certain constant amount of growth potential, which we can control by pruning; herein lies a good deal of the "secret" of pruning. In certain cases however two methods of pruning can be used and this will be better understood by the following example.

Let us imagine that we have planted a large bed with a single rose variety, for example, 40–50 plants of the beautiful, scented Super Star. In the middle of March, if the weather is suitable, we start pruning and remove about two-thirds or more of all the branches produced during the previous summer, but we do this only to every alternate bush. On the remaining bushes we prune away only about one-third of the corresponding branches, unless they have been frosted further down. When all the bushes start to flower during June the lightly pruned plants will bloom first and produce many side-shoots with relatively small flowers, whereas the more severely pruned roses will flower later and give very few, but large blooms on long stems.

By varying the pruning programme in this way, the flowering period will be prolonged, giving

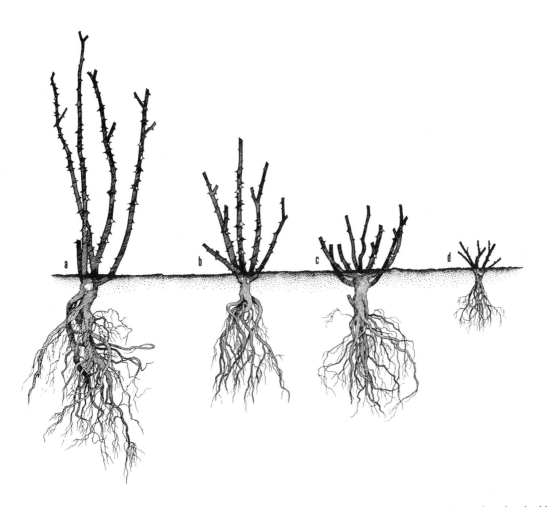

At pruning time in March, always remove very thin or completely dead twigs. The remaining sound, vigorous branches should then be pruned more or less severely according to the type of rose. The plant, (a), is a hybrid perpetual type which has very vigorous growth and mainly flowers on quite short branches. The thick, robust main branches should not therefore be cut back, if they are healthy, but should merely be shortened a little. The thinner lateral twigs should be cut back to a length of 2–4 inches and after some years a few very old and more or less exhausted branches can be removed completely. Plants (b) and (c) are hybrid tea roses, showing moderate and severe pruning respectively. The moderately pruned plant, (b), is a vigorous variety – for example Peace – which must not be pruned too hard every year as this will reduce the number of flowers produced; (c) shows how the majority of hybrid teas should be pruned every spring, after all the dead and weak twigs have been removed first. Furthermore, with a rose bed consisting entirely of one variety, every alternate plant can be pruned as (b), the others as (c). The plants of the b-type will then flower early with short-stemmed blooms, and those of the c-type later with long-stemmed blooms. Rose (d) shows the hard pruning required by many floribunda roses. The vigorous varieties of this group should be pruned less severely than in (d). (See also drawings, pp. 76–77).

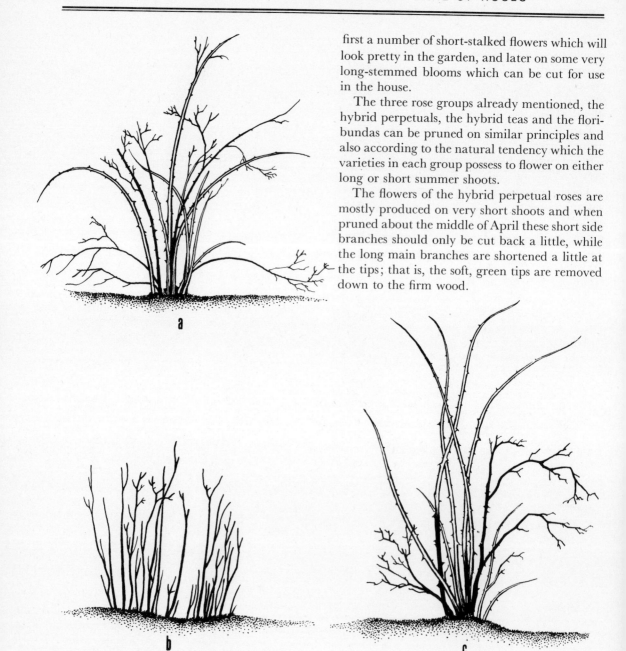

first a number of short-stalked flowers which will look pretty in the garden, and later on some very long-stemmed blooms which can be cut for use in the house.

The three rose groups already mentioned, the hybrid perpetuals, the hybrid teas and the floribundas can be pruned on similar principles and also according to the natural tendency which the varieties in each group possess to flower on either long or short summer shoots.

The flowers of the hybrid perpetual roses are mostly produced on very short shoots and when pruned about the middle of April these short side branches should only be cut back a little, while the long main branches are shortened a little at the tips; that is, the soft, green tips are removed down to the firm wood.

The shrub roses on these pages are the same as those shown on pages 86–87. The drawings show how shrub roses should be pruned, or more correctly, how they should be thinned out every second or third year. Close examination of the two drawings will show that a proportion of the shoots should be pruned right down to the ground. There is never any question of a true

In addition to this pruning all dead branches should be removed down to the living wood; this is recognisable by the bark being smooth and often green, or it will appear green when carefully scraped with a sharp knife. Very soft and thin, slightly pendulous twigs should also be removed.

Formerly these hybrid perpetual roses were pruned much too severely and the result was a series of long summer shoots which only produced very few, late flowers.

The hybrid teas flower on summer shoots of varying lengths and the pruning is carried out as follows: quite moderate pruning if we want many flowers with short stems and more severe if we want extra large, long-stemmed flowers (see drawing, p. 75). Dead and weak branches are removed as in the case of the hybrid perpetuals.

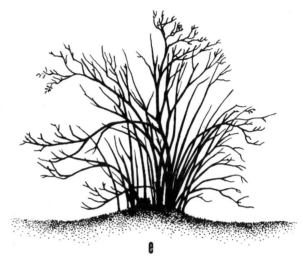

e

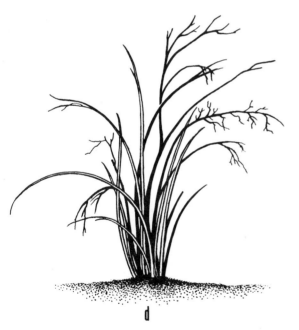

d

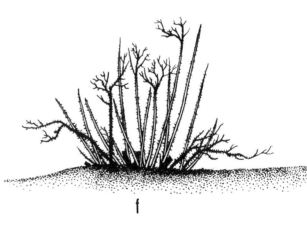

f

pruning of the young shoots as in the highly bred roses. At the most it is sufficient to snip off the unripe tips of last year's shoots, and as already mentioned, to remove the oldest branches right down to the ground. For this job, strong, long-shafted secateurs will prove useful.

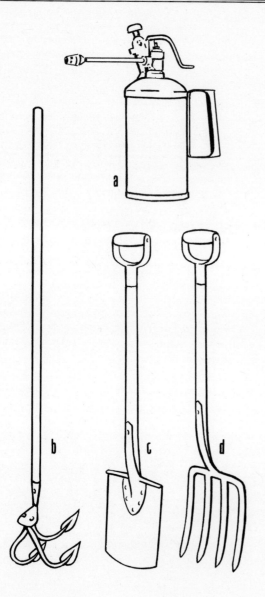

The rose grower's tools should be kept in good order. The main items required are: a. automatic hand spray with a capacity of about 2 pints of water or spray; b. hand cultivator to loosen the soil between the plants; c. spade; and d. fork.

Of the groups mentioned, the floribunda roses are the ones which flower most freely on long summer shoots, and which therefore tolerate severe pruning in April, without endangering the flowering in June. What we mean by severe pruning is shown best in the drawing on page 75. Furthermore there are certain varieties within this group, such as Poulsen's Bedder, Frensham and Märchenland which can be pruned right down to the ground, particularly if the plants are growing in the form of a large, broad hedge.

Finally, some mention should be made of the pruning of climbers and shrub roses, even if this has already been briefly mentioned.

Let us choose two widely different types of climbing roses, Dorothy Perkins and Gloire de Dijon, of which the flowers are shown in colour plates 55 and 56; the reader is also asked to refer to the drawing on page 88. Dorothy Perkins belongs among the small-flowered climbing roses and the numerous small blooms are produced in large clusters on very long, thin, bright green shoots.

Gloire de Dijon has large, double flowers growing singly or at the most a couple at a time on short side branches from the shoots.

When the Dorothy Perkins type is several years old, the plant will send up several vigorous, young shoots from the ground (these are not suckers) and by July–August many of these will be six feet long and valuable because they will carry next year's flowers. So when the older branches have finished flowering in the course of August, it will be in order to prune down to the ground some of the 2–3-year-old branches that have flowered and gradually to tie up the young shoots. This should be done with large loops on the ties, for each shoot will still grow considerably, both in length and thickness, and the tighter the tie, the more likely is the shoot to break.

After this severe summer pruning, the plant is left with a number of young summer shoots and also a few young branches which have flowered; the flower clusters with numerous withered blooms can be quite simply removed with the secateurs.

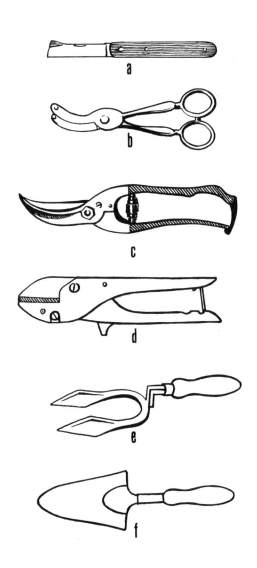

The most important small tools are: a. a budding knife, specially shaped for budding; b. a special type of secateurs for cutting roses; c. for pruning – the so-called "double-shears" are the best, but the most expensive; d. a cheaper type which can be used; e. a strong hand fork which is used to keep the soil loose between the roses; f. a hand trowel to plant annuals between the rose bushes.

Unlike other roses this climber will not require any severe pruning in March, if the thinning-out just described has been undertaken in the previous autumn; but the young shoots which were tied to the espalier will scarcely have become properly ripened and so each one should be cut back to firm, ripe wood. If there are dead branches and twigs following a strong frost, these should be completely removed. All the ties should be examined, and if necessary renewed, but there is no need to tie back each individual little branch to the wall or post. Here and there allow some small branches to hang free in the air, thus accentuating the grace and beauty of this attractive climber.

The large-flowered climbers (Gloire de Dijon type) are pruned in the course of March to about the same extent as a vigorous hybrid tea type or like a hybrid perpetual, but this is only done after the shoots, with the help of suitable ties, have adequately covered the surface of the wall or wooden fence. In this type the shoots should be allowed to grow for several years, and so some thought should be given to the positions in which they are tied to the wall when young. Now and again, very vigorous upright shoots may grow out from these older, more or less oblique branches, and if there is space these fast-growing, sappy shoots can be tied to the wall or espalier, taking care that the ties are not too tight. As already mentioned, these climbers are pruned in much the same way as the ordinary large-flowered garden roses and it is essential not to cut off too much of the younger, very short side branches, provided they are healthy and ripe – that is, when they have smooth green or brownish-green bark and small firm buds.

In general, the lateral branches from the previous year should be pruned down to a length of 4–10 inches. In practice, this means that if the branches are firm and ripe, one only cuts back the extreme tip until a firm bud is reached. In later years, old, large-flowered climbers can to a certain extent be rejuvenated. This is done by judiciously cutting back large, exhausted branches just above a vigorous side shoot or by removing them right down to the ground. But this type of rejuvenation should only be done at intervals of several years. These two types of climbing rose are shown on page 88 and the reader himself must now try to place the many beautiful varieties between these two extremes and allow common sense to determine whether pruning is done according to one method or the other.

The shrub or bush roses, as previously mentioned, do not require much pruning, but a thinning-out every year or every second year will help to keep the bush vigorous and profusely flowering (see drawings, pp. 76–77 and 86–87).

The term, "thinning-out", is used to describe the removal of complete shoots right down to the ground and of badly placed branches which cross or obstruct the younger stems. As a general principle it is best to respect a shrub rose and to destroy as little as possible of its natural form. This is particularly important if some of the branches hang over gracefully, or if the growth is stiff and erect this characteristic should also be preserved.

It is usually said that rejuvenation should take place annually or at intervals of 2–3 years, by removing 3–5 old, exhausted shoots which can be easily recognised by their coarser bark and numerous half-withered twigs at the top. As already mentioned, such branches should be pruned right down to the ground with strong, long-shafted secateurs and it is advisable to wear strong leather gloves when doing this.

The young, long, overhanging shoots, which usually have several small side shoots, must not be pruned – apart from perhaps removing their soft, unripe tips, as is done with the climbing roses.

Shrub roses can be pruned during mild periods in the winter and right on until the end of March, and there is nothing wrong in removing a few old branches after a period of profuse flowering in June–July, for it appears that the younger shoots need more light and air.

But one can also wait until the autumn to prune such old shoots which should by then be carrying a mass of beautiful hips that will be appreciated for house decoration.

Disease and pests

Several diseases and pests attack roses and the most important of these will be described in the following pages.

FUNGUS DISEASES

Rose mildew is the commonest of these diseases and at the same time the most difficult to combat. The attacks appear as white coatings on the green parts of the plant, mainly at the tips of the shoots, on leaves, petioles and flower buds. It prevents the young shoots from developing naturally, and they become deformed.

Rose mildew differs from other fungal diseases in that it thrives best in warm, dry weather, and so is worst on climbing roses on south walls and on roses which stand in a draught.

There is considerable variation in the resistance of the different varieties, but as a general rule the smooth-leaved forms fight the disease most successfully.

Rose mildew must be combated throughout the summer, preferably by means of a weekly treatment with one of the compounds mentioned in the table on page 83.

It is also worth noting that this fungus over-winters on the rose plants, and so it may be treated during the resting period. Spraying with 10% lime sulphur just before the buds burst will be a good basis for attaining a successful result.

Black spot appears as dark spots which radiate out from a central point. The spots later become black and more or less run together, so that they may cover most of the leaf surface. An attack causes damage because the plants lose a proportion of their foliage at a premature stage, and it may affect reproduction and hardiness, thus causing significant debilitation.

It should be combated during the summer by means of an active substance (see table, p. 83), by collecting up all fallen leaves, and also by carefully cleaning the spaces between plants, so that infected leaves do not lie about through the winter.

Rose rust appears in the spring as an orange-coloured powder on branches, shoots and stems; in the summer orange spots, which later turn black, appear on the undersides of the leaves.

Here again there is considerable variation in the resistance of the different varieties. Tea roses, polyantha roses, climbers and many hybrid teas are resistant.

Treatment must start before the buds burst in the spring, by cutting off any parts of the plant that show yellow spots, after they have been painted over with alcohol or fruit-tree carbolineum to prevent the spread of the disease. In the case of an attack in summer the plants should be sprayed with a zineb substance.

Stem canker (Stem fungus) One often sees a single bud drooping and this can happen to leaf and flower buds; there will also be dead parts on the stem below the bud.

This can be caused by various fungal diseases and it seems best to remove the affected part of the shoot.

Protection against the attack can be obtained by spraying with fungicides, and as the same substances act as preventives of the foregoing diseases this will not give any extra trouble.

PESTS

Aphids Like most other plants, roses are attacked by various species of plant-lice or aphids which cause deformity and weakness by sucking the young parts of the plant.

It is important that action be taken as soon as the attack is observed, for if the first insects are allowed to spread, it may be difficult to master them (see table, p. 83). Winter spraying with Abol X can be advantageous after summers with severe attacks.

Rose beetles are small pale green insects which suck at the undersides of the leaves and cause the well-known yellowish-white spotting of the leaves particularly along the main veins. The insects may be very difficult to detect, but one usually finds white, moulted larval skins in large numbers, thus disclosing the source of the attack.

Even though the leaves seldom fall off as a result, active measures are necessary because the insects cause much weakening. Some of the substances used against aphids will also act on these beetles.

Thrips are very small black insects which live inside the flower buds and cause brown spots on the petals, and an attack may be so serious that the flower buds are completely deformed or their development stopped. This pest can be controlled by D.D.T.

Red spiders attack roses out in the open now and again but are more common in greenhouses. They are very small spider-like animals which suck at the undersides of the leaves and cause these to become grey-brown.

Action should be taken if there is any suspicion of an attack, as otherwise the plants may be severely weakened. The substance used is malathion.

Caterpillars The larvae of various small moths bind the leaves together with their silk and eat them. An attack may be very serious and can be controlled by spraying with D.D.T., though picking by hand is best.

Leaf-rolling sawfly The larvae of certain sawflies attack roses in various ways: a young shoot may grow lop-sided because the sawfly has laid eggs in one side of it; in other cases the leaves are skeletonised and one species causes the leaves to roll together from the edge; larvae of the rose-shoot sawfly hollow out the young shoots which then wither.

In the latter case there is nothing to do but cut off the attacked shoots; the other attacks, however, can be controlled by appropriate spraying or dusting.

Hip flies An attack by the larvae of the hip fly can be very annoying if the hips are being grown for jam or for some other reason.

The white larvae, which are about $\frac{1}{2}$ inch long, gnaw into the flesh of the hip and render it useless.

They can usually be controlled by repeated spraying with a D.D.T. preparation in July–August.

Bugs Several kinds of bugs gnaw holes in the green leaves, one of the most dangerous being the larvae of the capsid bugs. Bugs may be difficult to control for they are nocturnal insects which hide away during the day and are seldom seen. Control measures must therefore cover not only the infected plants but also bushes and trees in the vicinity, not forgetting hedges which are an excellent hiding-place for these pests. Use Dipterex and malathion.

Gall wasps mainly attack wild roses and cause the formation of strongly lobed parts on the shoots. There is no method of control apart from cutting off the attacked parts of the plant.

VIRUSES

Various virus diseases can be observed on roses – for example, *yellow mosaic*, which manifests itself as a yellow coloration along the main veins of the leaves.

Virus diseases are transmitted from one generation to the next with material for propagation or they may be transferred from one plant to another by sucking insects such as aphids, which must therefore be kept under control. There is no way of stopping a virus disease once it has begun and one must therefore ensure that purchased plants are healthy. Seriously affected bushes should be burned.

CONTROL MATERIALS

The adjoining table shows the substances which can be used against the different pests and fungal diseases.

The terms used to describe these compounds are group names, each of which covers a number of special preparations. In most cases, the substances within each group are used in the same way.

Instructions regarding dosage and any necessary safety precautions are given with each package.

As will be seen there is no single compound which will cover everything, so in each case one has to select the agent most suitable for the case in hand. There are certain mixtures which contain two or more of the active substances and in practice it often pays to use these.

It is very rare for a single substance to be active against both pests and fungal diseases, and among the agents mentioned in the table only white oil fulfils this function.

TABLE OF FUNGICIDES AND INSECTICIDES

Substance used

	DDT	Lindan	Malathion	Sulphur thiram	White oil	Zineb	Captan (orthocide)
Rose mildew				+	+		
Black spot						+	+
Rose rust						+	
Stem canker				+		+	+
Aphids		+	+				
Rose beetles	+	+	+				
Thrips	+	+					
Red spider			+		+		
Caterpillars	+	+	+				
Leaf-rolling Sawfly	+	+					
Hip flies	+						
Bugs	+		+				

In addition to the substances named in the table there are a few others which are of interest in special cases.

As already mentioned, *lime sulphur* is used before the buds burst as a spray against mildew.

Finally we may mention the dusting agent, Pirox, which is of value against rose pests and diseases; besides controlling fungal diseases such as mildew and black spot it is also active against certain pests.

METHODS OF TREATING DISEASE

In practice it is nearly always necessary to carry out control operations against disease.

One can choose between two methods: spraying and dusting – though there are a few cases where the substance in question does not lend itself to either method.

Both methods are perfectly satisfactory, but it should be made clear that if dusting is chosen – it is the easier of the two – then twice as many applications will be needed as in the case of spraying.

There is also a difference in method of procedure according to whether one is dealing with fungal diseases or with insect pests. In the case of fungal disease the measures are designed to protect the plants against attack. This means that the plants have to be covered the whole time with a fine layer of the protective material, and treatment has thus to be repeated at least once every two weeks throughout the growth period in order to give sufficient protection against diseases such as mildew and black spot.

Control of pests can be started after an attack has been observed, but it may be extremely important for treatment to be prompt, as many of these insects have a disconcerting capacity for breeding very fast.

It is unfortunate that nearly all the substances used to protect roses cause a greater or lesser amount of spotting. White oil is one of the few substances which does not do this to any extent.

Roses in the garden

When one thinks of the depressing rose beds with box hedges and the roses in neat rows that adorned the formal gardens of the Victorian era, one can have more sympathy for the professional gardener who suggested that roses should be hidden away in the kitchen garden.

But nowadays, the use of roses in the garden has become less stereotyped, partly because we have much better varieties and partly because our whole outlook on the design and appearance of gardens has changed; symmetry, "axes" and geometrical drawing-board designs have almost disappeared and gardens are now designed on much freer principles.

Today garden plants, and roses in particular, form a natural part of the plant landscape, which may consist of profusely flowering perennials, colourful annuals or pretty evergreen bushes and low, creeping green plants with delicate foliage. Turning to roses we may indeed be content with growing a couple of attractive ramblers on the balcony or perhaps filling a wooden tub with a few profusely flowering, scented roses and placing it in a warm place close to the house. A few rows of fine roses for cutting can be planted in the kitchen garden, for a couple of full, scented roses on the breakfast table are as much of a psychological tonic as vitamin pills are a physical boost. But one ought to lay out a complete little rose garden, in a warm place open to the sun, where the colour, form and scent of the roses can become an unforgettable experience throughout the whole of the summer.

Finally, all the new and old bush or shrub roses should be mentioned. These can be used to form attractive, flowering hedges around a country cottage garden or they can be planted individually around green lawns to show off properly their grace and profusion of flowering.

There are many sides to the whole idea of *Roses in the garden* and the possibilities are so varied that it is worth dividing the subject up into sections.

Let us therefore begin with something on shrub roses and the old-fashioned roses which only bloom once a year.

SHRUB ROSES AND THEIR USE IN THE GARDEN

Shrub roses have the following characteristics in common: very vigorous growth, in some cases up to 9–12 ft in height and breadth. There is therefore no question of their being used in beds like ordinary garden roses.

They are mostly grown on their own roots, that is the roots and the top of the plant belong to the same individual in contrast to the "improved" roses in which the top or scion is budded on to a wild root.

Shrub roses usually only flower once in June–July, but new varieties and species are constantly coming on the market which, by hybridisation with long-flowering roses, will bloom several times; the first flowering, however, is always the richest. As a rule shrub roses do not require annual pruning like the highly selected garden roses, but will be content with a rigorous thinning-out at intervals of 2–4 years (see drawing and text, pp. 76–77 and 86–87).

Shrub roses can be used in a variety of ways and to get an idea of these it is best to divide them into a couple of groups according to their growth habits and preferred positions.

Mention should first be made of those shrub roses which have compact, twiggy growth, sometimes with underground runners.

Several of these bushes form tight, compact shrubs in the course of a few years. This applies amongst others to *R. rugosa*, *R. spinosissima*, *R. Carolina* and *R. virginiana*, which are particularly suitable for planting on slopes and for forming compact shelter hedges around summerhouses and similar places. They should be planted quite close together, for example three feet apart in both directions. During the first two years the soil around should be kept clean with a fork and

Rosa moyesii

Rosa willmottiae

a hand cultivator, but it should not be dug with a spade; the intention is to allow all the roots to have the chance of spreading out unhindered. In the course of 3–4 years, one will have a dense, impenetrable mass of plants which will act as a shelter against the wind.

Other shrub roses have a graceful growth form and many produce long, overhanging branches full of attractive flowers, which are followed by shiny red hips. Growth may also be very compact and erect as in the old-fashioned moss roses, centifolia roses and Provence roses which flowered only once a year. In both cases, however, the characteristic and very graceful form should be allowed to develop into its full beauty. They should not be planted too close together, and in some cases they ought to stand free on a grassy lawn or at the most surrounded by plants of low, compact growth.

The old-fashioned shrub roses, such as Maiden's Blush, Louise Odier, Boule de Neige and others which were so popular in our great-grandmothers' gardens are particularly suitable today for planting around country cottages.

These roses will produce a far more romantic atmosphere with their grace and fine scent, than all the so-called antique wrought-iron lamps, well-heads and so on which people use as rustic accessories.

Among the vigorous growing shrub roses with long, graceful, overhanging branches the roses, Frühlingsmorgen, Nevada, and Rustica deserve a special mention; of the older ones, *R. hugonis*,

R. moyesii and *R. rubrifolia* are some of the most beautiful plants in a group that is rich in species and varieties.

Do not, however, be tempted to plant too many of them. Choose a few specimens and plant them out on the lawn either singly or in groups of three to five, so that each one or each group has ample space all round to show off its good points. In practice this means that each bush needs a circular area with a diameter of about 6–9 ft.

These beautiful relatives of our native wild roses can be used to form loose bushy areas on the outskirts of the garden, but they are perhaps best underplanted with low-growing flowering plants and dwarf bushes.

The plants to be used for this purpose should fit in well with the roses; they should be un-obtrusive, should not have the appearance of being too sophisticated and their size should be in keeping with the dimensions of the garden.

The following examples may be mentioned: *Potentilla fruticosa* with all its varieties, *Stephanandra incisa crispa*, *Vinca minor*, *Epimedium hybrida*, *Cotoneaster horizontalis* and *Cotoneaster dammeri*.

In conclusion, we must not forget that shrub roses produce beautiful fruits, known colloquially as hips, of which a selection is shown in colour (plate 1).

The first impact of seeing a rose bush the height of a man, smothered with bright sealing-wax-red hips and half covered with small white caps of snow, is such that inevitably one wants it to have a permanent place in the garden. *R. rubrifolia*

(Copper Rose) is a good example of this.

And finally we should not forget that the dense thickets made by shrub roses are much favoured by song birds as nest sites.

CLIMBING ROSES AND RAMBLERS

Sometimes the roses in this group are also called "creeping" roses, and this term is really more correct than those given in the above sub-title because they are not equipped with tendrils, adhesive aerial roots, nor do their stems entwine. But it is probably more practical to refer to them here as climbers and ramblers which are the terms used to describe all the roses which produce long stems.

Under natural conditions, the original wild forms of these climbing roses are large mound-like thickets, each a wilderness of long, thin branches which cascade down over gentle slopes. These branches then touch the ground, take root and

Shrub roses are usually most attractive when they have plenty of space to develop in. This will be seen from the drawings which show the height and width of fully developed bushes, which may grow higher than a man. The roses, Nevada, Frühlingsmorgen, and R. rustica have a broad, slightly pendulous habit (a), whereas R. spinosissima and R. rugosa have a compact, twiggy growth and numerous underground runners (b). R. rugosa and R. eglanteria grow tall and loosely (c). R. hugonis (d)

again produce thin, creeping lianas 3 feet or more long, thus eventually covering several square yards of ground.

The cultivated climbing roses, hybrids between the vigorous wild forms and some of the large-flowered garden roses, have this kind of growth to a greater or lesser extent; they also have beautiful, large, scented flowers. In this group one extreme is represented by the so-called ramblers, vigorous climbing roses with relatively thin shoots, up to 9–18 feet long, and very small scentless flowers in compact clusters as in the rambler roses (for example, Dorothy Perkins, American Pillar, Excelsa). This type of rose only flowers once in the season. We can call these roses "the bouquet flowering climbers".

The other extreme among the climbing roses is illustrated by the ordinary large-flowered hybrid tea roses, of which some have varieties (sports or mutants) with such vigorous growth

e

d

f

produces attractive, graceful, slightly overhanging bushes, and the old-fashioned R. alba (e) grows into a compact, slightly pendulous bush. The lovely rugosa hybrid rose, Dagmar Hastrup (f) has compact, low, broad growth. For instructions on pruning these shrub roses, see the drawings on pages 76–77.

The climbing roses can be divided into two main groups. This drawing shows (left) the appearance of the large-flowered, some-what stiff-branched climbing roses alongside the more vigorous, small-flowered ramblers with thinner branches and very long shoots. The large-flowered varieties should be only lightly pruned every year, almost as for the hybrid perpetual roses. The small-flowered varieties should be pruned or thinned out annually by removing a few of the old, exhausted branches right down to the ground and allowing plenty of space for the young green branches to be tied up. This can be done immediately after the end of flowering.

that they can only be cultivated in ordinary beds with difficulty and have to be tied to walls, fences or pergola supports. The English call these roses "Climbers", and in books and catalogues they are denoted as Climbing Peace, Climbing Mme. Caroline Testout, Climbing Sutter's Gold and so on. In these climbing forms the flowers are exactly the same as in the parent variety; they only differ in their form of growth which is very vigorous,

producing long stems.

Between these two extremes in growth form and flowering there are various intermediates; new climbing varieties have been produced, particularly during recent years, which unite strong, vigorous growth with profuse production until right into late summer of large flowers of the hybrid tea type.

The most vigorous of the climbing roses are best suited for positions where they can spread out and produce an abundance of flowers. One can hide tall wooden fences or allow the roses to grow freely over the roof of a pergola or of a garden shed. On old houses the roses can be led up to a balcony above a veranda or a bay-window.

One can embed an old curved branch firmly in the ground or make a light, but strong, framework of bamboo or oak stakes and plant a couple of climbing roses at the foot and let their shoots grow freely and unhampered up among the branches or through the frame so that they finish up in the air with branches full of lovely roses hanging freely.

It is obvious that the shoots must be loosely tied to a fence or trellis at the beginning, but the secret is to allow as many branches as possible to

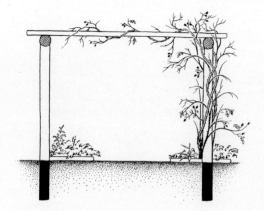

A pergola provides an attractive and appropriate site for many kinds of climbing rose. Always use very thick, pressure-impregnated posts and thinner horizontals (respectively 6–8 inches and 3–5 inches in diameter), and make the width of the pergola greater than its height, e.g. 9 feet and 7 feet.

hang freely and gracefully, thus evoking profuse flowering and the maximum of grace.

The large-flowered, scented, climbing roses have a more moderate growth and they should be used slightly differently from the vigorous climbing roses mentioned above. Perhaps they are most beautiful when grown neatly in the form of an espalier up a wall or wooden shelter, or fence, and best of all when they are grown together with large-flowered, blue *Clematis*.

But care should be taken with the colours. Bright, dark red climbing roses, such as the variety Blaze, do not look well against a red brick wall; pale pink roses grown in proximity would, for instance, be a most unfortunate combination, which colour-conscious people would find quite repulsive. (More detailed notes on the problems of colour combinations and some suggestions for plants which go well with roses are given on page 97; a full explanation of the pruning and care of climbing roses is given in the text and drawings on pages 77 and 78.)

Whereas the large-flowered climbing roses are best grown up against a wall or wooden fence, the vigorous, small-flowered ramblers require more space; their large flower-clusters should preferably hang free in the air. For example, this drawing shows an attractive garden seat which will have acquired a vigorous roof of hanging climbers in the course of a couple of years.

ORDINARY LOW-GROWING GARDEN ROSES: HYBRID PERPETUALS, HYBRID TEAS AND FLORIBUNDAS

The roses in these groups are all "improved". This means that they are propagated in such a way that each plant consists of a "wild" rootstock and a "selected" top, these two parts having grown together after the operation known as budding.

Furthermore all the roses in these groups flower profusely and several times during the season; most of them are relatively low-growing – from 20–30 inches in height, although some grow to 40 inches and a few to 60 inches. They are all suitable for planting in large or small beds or grouped together in special rose gardens.

In short, they are highly cultivated, very beautiful garden plants and they should be used as such.

Let us now examine them one group at a time, starting with the first-named and oldest, the hybrid perpetual, or remontant, roses. These originated from the hybridisation of newly introduced rose species (see p. 53) about the beginning of the last century. They quickly gained admittance to the gardens of our great-great-grandparents, which had previously had only a relatively small number of moss roses, centifolia roses, Provence roses and others, all of which only flowered once in each season.

The words remontant and perpetual mean that these roses flower two or more times in the course of the summer and as they have large, well-filled, strongly scented blooms, they soon became widely distributed in nineteenth-century gardens. Growth is robust and tall, and the flowers usually appear on short branches, which themselves spring from long, stiff, erect shoots.

Nowadays the old varieties such as the white Frau Karl Druschki (Snow Queen), the dark red Hugh Dickson and the cherry-red Ulrich Brunner

The "improved" roses can be divided into three main groups: the hybrid perpetuals, the hybrid teas and floribunda roses. This separation is sometimes difficult to define sharply, because some rose varieties, by crossing within the three groups, come to resemble one group just as much as another. Nevertheless, experts are agreed that the division into groups is useful. This drawing shows the growth form of different roses. The oldest of the groups, the hybrid perpetuals (a) have tall, erect growth and, as can be seen, reach almost to shoulder height on a man. The hybrid teas (b) are on the average scarcely as tall as the hybrid perpetuals and have a somewhat broader, bushy growth – to about hip height. The floribunda roses may have vigorous, erect growth (c), but certain varieties in this group have low, spreading growth (d). See drawing on page 75 for the pruning of these roses.

and others have almost, I suppose, a certain nostalgic value. Elderly gardeners feel old memories revived by owning bushes of these roses which were surpassed long ago by new, profusely flowering, scented hybrid tea roses.

Nowadays, the next group, the hybrid teas, contains by far the largest number of modern garden roses and also the most valuable.

These roses have mainly arisen by hybridisation between hybrid perpetual and tea roses, but other rose species and varieties have also contributed to the rich variety of form and colour to be

Frau Karl Druschki

found in this group's immensely rich assortment.

Whereas the flowers of the hybrid perpetual roses are often broadly spherical in shape and a little heavy and rustic, those of most of the hybrid teas are very elegant and refined. The flowers, which grow singly or in twos or threes together on long stems, are slender and pointed when in bud, and when half open the petals stand gracefully arranged in a spiral running towards the centre, the outermost with their edges gracefully recurved, giving a beautiful play of colour.

The leaves are often glossy and dark green, and in many varieties, the young shoots are red-brown or dark purplish-red.

The scent of the flowers varies from one variety to the next but many have inherited the fine tea-rose scent of their ancestors (see the list, p. 103).

Details on the planting and pruning of the hybrid tea roses will be found on pages 72–77.

The floribunda roses, the last of the three main groups of low-growing garden roses, were once known as hybrid polyantha or bouquet roses. These three names all denote the main characteristic of the group: the flowers are carried several together in large or small clusters, or bouquets.

The individual flowers in the clusters may indeed be just as large, well-filled and beautifully shaped as those of the hybrid teas, but it is more usual for the clusters to consist of small, semi-double flowers which seen together give the effect of a series of large, bright splashes of colour.

Most of the flowers in this group are scentless, but among the newer varieties there are some with a scent just as fragrant as in the hybrid teas (see the list, p. 103).

The origin and history of the floribunda roses are discussed on page 55 and their planting and pruning on pages 72–77.

THE PLACE OF THE ROSE AND ITS USE IN THE GARDEN

At the beginning of this chapter it was mentioned that a generation or two ago many horticulturalists, garden architects and so on were not particularly well-disposed towards roses, which they considered should be kept in the kitchen garden. They wanted the garden to be green and vigorous, without paths, symmetry and artificial arrangements and in particular they wanted the naked earth between roses and other bushes to be inconspicuous. Moreover, one could scarcely say that the lanky rose bushes looked anything special, especially during winter and far on into the spring. In summer they would often be plagued by mildew and aphids, and disease left very few really beautiful and faultless roses.

And so the tendency was for gardens to have lovely wide green lawns, several good conifers, rare, leafy evergreen shrubs, and everywhere outside the lawns the ground was covered from hedge to hedge by a carpet of evergreen plants. Gardens deliberately began to be lush, peaceful green oases in the big city's suburban areas.

It was also noticeable, however, that many gardeners began gradually to feel the need for colour, flowers and scent, for even though most gardens today have a richly varied assortment of spring flowers, the summer may well give the appearance of being rather poor in colour and scent.

Nowadays roses have been improved in so many ways that they must be reckoned the most valuable of all garden flowers; and we should remember that a garden full of roses could never be accused of being poor in colour or scent.

Modern roses should, however, be used quite differently from the way in which they were used in the older gardens.

Under no circumstances should we return to the long, narrow, very dismal rose beds with box hedges out on the lawn, or to the sad, sunbaked beds along the foot of the house, facing south or west, which were most unsuitable for roses. The circular rose bed in the middle of the lawn at the foot of the flagstaff should also be a thing of the past – and any surviving relics quickly abandoned. In the gardens of today there are three main possibilities for the effective use of roses.

First we can have a few regular, closely planted rose beds in a sunny place on the lawn if this is sufficiently large. In addition to or as an alternative to this we can have roses as the dominant theme in a special rose garden, and anyone who owns a comparatively small terrace-house garden can convert the whole of this into a rose garden with some good seats and a few attractive, evergreen bushes which will give the garden a sheltered and cosy appearance in the wintertime.

Finally, roses can be used to give an element of colour among evergreen bushes and conifers and in special cases suitable varieties can be planted among perennials and rock plants.

The following good advice can also be given concerning rose beds on the lawn:

The beds ought to be of a suitable size, quite apart from whether they are square, rectangular, hexagonal or circular in shape. They should not be under 3 feet across nor more than $4\frac{1}{2}$ feet, and should therefore cover an area of $1–2\frac{1}{2}$ square yards.

If they are made larger they will appear too big in relation to the size of the lawn, and it will also be difficult to reach the centre of the bed for upkeep. If they are less than a square yard in area, the number of roses will be too small and the whole effect will appear skimpy.

These square or circular beds should be placed in a sunny position on the lawn, and to obtain the best possible colour effect from the roses it is a good idea to plant a simple background of dark green bushes (yew, bay, prunus lauroceracus, *Mahonia, Cotoneaster*). Secondly, one should, so far as possible, keep dark red, orange-red, yellow, pink, white and many-coloured rose varieties separate, each in its own bed. It is also best to place the pure, strong colour tones in the foreground and the pale, delicate tones nearest to the bushes in the background.

See also the section on colour combinations in the rose garden (p. 97), and the adjoining drawings of suggested layouts for a rose garden.

Grass borders between the rose beds should not be less than 30–36 inches wide; if they are narrower they become too difficult to maintain and the green background colour – so valuable in among the multi-coloured roses – will be too weak. It is extremely important to have a tranquil green carpet of grass to neutralise the clash of colours inevitably evoked by the roses, when so many bright colours are placed close to each other.

On practical grounds the beds can be edged with paving stones at the rate of 5 pieces to the yard. Narrow strips of grey cement can also be used, but care should be taken that the edges never become too dominating; perhaps the best edging is black

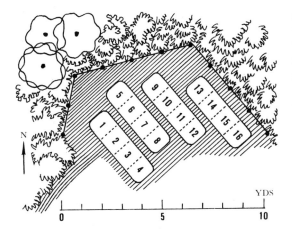

This plan shows the layout of a special garden for growing roses intended for cutting. It can have long, regular beds which are easy of access. The following are recommended as scented varieties which are especially suitable for cutting: 1. Iceberg, 2. Columbine, 3. Allgold, 4. Irene of Denmark, 5. Pink Peace, 6. Grace de Monaco, 7. Queen Elizabeth, 8. Virgo, 9. Texas Centennial, 10. Sutter's Gold, 11. Tiffany, 12. Geheimrat Duisberg, 13. Super Star, 14. Chrysler Imperial, 15. Hanne, 16. Ama.

clinker, or narrow strips of black cement, but these are expensive. Further details on soil treatment and planting are given on page 68.

The rose garden The really ideal garden, which both amateur gardener and expert dream about, consists of a single, large green lawn enclosed by tall hedges or walls – against all the neighbours – so that a man can really have privacy during his leisure.

Here and there flowering shrubs and an occasional tree rise up from the peaceful expanse of green to give the garden a truly picturesque beauty and the possibility of the rich interplay of light and shade. The perennials, roses and annuals are grouped together in small beds through which one can saunter at leisure. The advantage of such beds is that one can preserve the green harmony of the garden and also see the flowers in a smaller area, so that they look more attractive and striking to the observer. Furthermore, insofar

as roses are concerned, the scent of the flowers will be accentuated when they are grouped together or protected behind low hedges or close fences so that it will not be dissipated by the slightest puff of wind.

At one time such rose gardens, or rosaria as they were called, were laid out as separate units in the garden, but nowadays it is clearly realised how important it is in our blustery climate to have some kind of shelter for both man and his roses. Such a rose garden is really a latter-day cloister garden or refuge whither one can retreat for an hour or two to dream and meditate among scented roses and beautiful lilies.

The possibilities for placing a rosarium in the modern garden are many. It can, for example, be put in direct communication with the house, to the south or west, and regarded as a big open-air room, equipped with a large, covered sitting-area and a small open one, from which the roses can be admired from a second viewpoint.

The house itself can form one side of the area, or two sides if it is L-shaped. The other sides (the rose garden need not necessarily be rectangular) can, if expense is not of great importance, be made as a wall of brick or of breeze block. But the cheaper materials available nowadays are perfectly satisfactory, e.g. cane fencing or chestnut paling provided that the upright stakes have been impregnated under pressure.

Living enclosures of hedges or climbing plants on galvanised wire-netting can also be used, but with this method it takes a little longer before the area is properly enclosed.

Whether the sides of the rose garden consist of brickwork or fences, they should preferably be enlivened and made more colourful by the use of various climbing plants.

This can be done by planting climbers with particularly attractive foliage, such as *Aristolochia*, *Lonicera Henryi* (evergreen honeysuckle), *Hedera helix* (common ivy) or *Parthenocissus*, but experience shows that very few gardeners have sufficient strength of character to be consistent, even though such a plan will give the roses the best and most tranquil background.

It is not possible to give hard and fast rules on the best way to divide up the rose garden into beds, paths and sitting-places, for this will always be dependent upon conditions on the spot and on purely personal wishes. The adjacent plans and drawings will perhaps give some ideas and the following brief points should serve as a general guide:

As recommended in the case of rose beds set in a lawn, the beds in a rosarium should be neither too large nor too small, so here again the largest size should be 2–3 yards square and never less than one yard square.

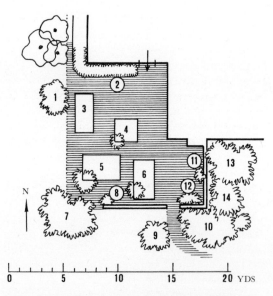

This plan shows how it is possible to convert a sheltered yard into a scented rose garden, with the roses planted in beds and also to form a frame around the garden. 1. Frühlingsmorgen, 2. bed with blue and violet annuals, 3. floribunda roses of the varieties Allgold, Lilli Marlene, Masquerade and Sarabande, 4. a whole bed of the variety Hanne, 5. a bed with the varieties Sutter's Gold, Super Star, Texas Centennial and Peace, 6. a bed with the varieties Queen Elizabeth, Pink Peace, Virgo and Spek's Yellow, 7. a group of 3–5 Nevada, 8. a climber, Golden Showers, 9. Maiden's Blush, 10. Stella Polaris and Dagmar Hastrup, 11. Danse des Sylphes, 12. Mrs. John Laing, 13. R. moyesii and R. helenae, 14. R. rubrifolia.

The actual shape of the beds is not of great significance, but it should preferably be kept quite simple and without too many unnecessary curves and edges; likewise very long, narrow beds are not attractive. Square, hexagonal or circular beds are always the best for an attractive rose garden.

The beds should be edged or framed with a material that is as unobtrusive as possible, e.g. as already mentioned, yellow brick-clinker, or quite low edging blocks of cement. If space allows the border can be of lavender, catmint, pinks and so on.

One can scarcely suggest box hedges nowadays, even though this edging plant is actually quite appropriate. The widespread use in churchyards over a couple of generations seems to have created an aversion to this little evergreen bush which is not easily overcome.

The paths and sitting-places should also be made of a material that is as neutral as possible, e.g. yellow clinker or small cement chips with rough surfaces. Perhaps the most attractive material would be pressure-impregnated wooden sleepers (old railway sleepers can be bought quite cheaply). Such a timber covering is very pleasant to walk on and looks attractive as a background for the roses. Cement garden chips in bright colours are not to be recommended under any circumstances.

After these general considerations on the walls of the garden, the shape of the beds, path surfaces and so on, it will be advisable to prepare a working plan of the rose garden, either on one's own or with a little assistance from an expert. This should be done on squared paper on a scale of 1:50 or 1:25 and an attempt should be made to place the varieties particularly favoured. Further details on the heights of different varieties, colour groups and so on are given on pages 103–106.

One problem which will probably arise immediately is whether to plant roses exclusively or to choose some other plants as company and background for the roses.

If a rose garden is planted exclusively with

roses it will look dismal and lifeless during the winter half of the year; it is easy to envisage how a few evergreen bushes would have an enlivening effect among the bare roses.

Although the removal of withered blooms and shoots has already been mentioned (page 73), it does no harm to point out that the appearance of the rose beds in winter will be greatly enhanced if this pruning is done during November–December. This is not a question of true pruning which is done in the spring, but merely of a little cleaning up to make the rose garden look tidy, even during the winter.

But let us return to the question of evergreen bushes among the rose beds. Here bushes such as *Ilex* (holly), *Cotoneaster salicifolia, Mahonia, Berberis stenophylla, Lonicera yunnanensis* and others will give the rose garden a certain cosy character in winter time, and furthermore they will always be useful in summer when something green is needed to put in among a bowl of cut roses. One can go further and plant particularly suitable perennials and rock plants, or even annuals, in some of the rose beds. On this point it is worth remembering that all plants with blue or violet-blue flowers will give attractive colour combinations and achieve a restful effect when combined with the rose's brilliant display of colour, most of which lies within the red and yellow part of the spectrum.

More will be said on the next page about this important aspect of rose-garden planting, namely the juxtaposition of colours and the selection of suitable neighbours for the rose.

At one time it was the custom to cover the ground between roses with plants such as *Cotula, Vinca, Cerastium, Acaena* and so on, but experience does not really support the use of these ground-covering plants, which make it difficult to loosen the soil between the roses and to add artificial manure; such plants must be very densely planted to give a good effect. However a close planting of low-growing plants along the edges of the rose beds can be recommended as a kind of compromise solution. So if one plants some clumps of chives, a few suitable perennials, some lilies and

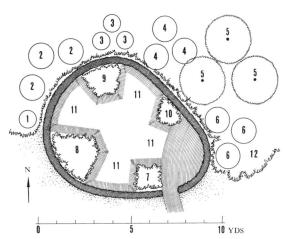

Even in a very small area the flower garden can be placed in a sunny corner, and this is much to be preferred to having small beds out on the lawn. This flower garden has a good shape; it can be enclosed by a low hedge of Ribes alpinum, large-leaved box or yew. A small paved area for sitting out can be made as shown on the right. A few attractive trees and bushes with scented flowers can be used as a backcloth to this small scented garden: *1*. Viburnum carlesii, *2. Maiden's Blush, 3.* Buddleia *Royal Red, 4.* Philadelphus *Virginal, 5.* Prunus padus *or* Crataegus *Paul's Scarlet, 6.* Syringa saugeana, *7. low floribunda roses, 8. tall hybrid teas, 9. low hybrid teas, 10. low floribunda roses, 11. low scented annuals and rock plants, e.g.* Alyssum benthani, Thymus serpyllum, Iris pumila, *etc., 12.* R. eglanteria.

annuals with here and there a single evergreen bush with character, one can create a very attractive and colourful scented rose garden, which will gladden the heart of its owner at all seasons. This is provided that the roses are thriving – with profuse flowering and vigorous, disease-free leaves and shoots – and this requires patience and good husbandry.

ROSES AMONG EVERGREEN BUSHES

In recent years, gardeners have shown considerable interest in evergreen, berry-bearing bushes and in conifers, and it is to be hoped that this

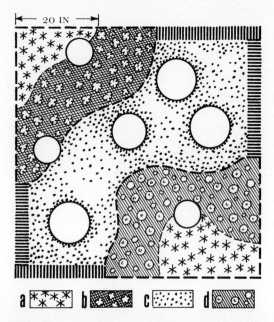

a ⁂   b ░   c ∴   d ◉

It is not always best to plant roses in beds by themselves, but care must be taken in choosing plants to grow with them. This drawing shows a square rose bed $4\frac{1}{2} \times 4\frac{1}{2}$ ft (or 6×6 ft) planted as follows. The large circles represent roses of the varieties Hanne and Super Star, the small circles the variety Lilli Marlene (3–5 plants in each circle). The underplanting can be: a. Thymus lanuginosus, b. Aubrietia Dr Mules, c. Aster King of the Dwarfs, d. Alyssum Violet Queen.

trend will continue. Our gardens will certainly gain in beauty and become less windy and greener in the winter than older gardens. The effect can sometimes become a little unrestful when too many evergreens with yellowish and bluish-green foliage are grouped together, so it is advisable to restrict the number of different varieties.

We cannot deal with these problems in greater detail in a book on roses but can recommend that a few groups of roses be placed with moderation and care among the evergreens.

If the gardener wishes to try this combination of roses and evergreen bushes, he must choose the most attractive neighbours for his roses. Among those that can be specially recommended are yew, holly, *Mahonia, Berberis candidula, Berberis*

verrucolosa, Berberis Julianae, Berberis stenophylla, large-leaved box, *Euonymus Fortunei vegeta, Lonicera pileata, Cotoneaster melanotricha, Cotoneaster microphylla* and others with glossy, dark green leaves which will all go well with the fresh foliage of the roses.

There are also certain rose varieties such as Irene of Denmark, Iceberg, Queen Elizabeth, Peace, Alain, Ama, Columbine, Frensham, Märchenland and Super Star, all with particularly attractive glossy leaves and good growth, which are very suitable for planting among evergreen shrubs. The latter will considerably enhance the accompanying roses.

Groups of 5–9 roses of a single variety planted really closely together so that they form a single bush will be the most appropriate. These large clumps can then be surrounded by low-growing evergreen ground plants, with the taller evergreen shrubs mentioned above being planted behind the roses and in between the clumps, but with a reasonable distance between each plant.

ROSES, PERENNIALS AND ANNUALS

When describing the planting of roses it was mentioned earlier that certain perennials and annuals go remarkably well with roses planted in beds.

One may well have insufficient space to have a rose garden as well as separate large beds for perennials and annuals, and yet may wish to have some of the latter two groups of flowers. Would it be unwise or perhaps quite disastrous to plant a few roses together with the perennials and annuals?

The answer to this is not a definite yes or no, because there are some perennials and annuals which definitely do not go well with large-flowered roses and where both the rose and the other flower would suffer by being seen in close proximity.

Try to imagine scarlet roses and orange marigolds together or pink roses close to bronze-red dahlias, not to mention perennial poppies, *Papaver orientale* or *Astilbe* alongside groups of

Peace

will nearly always look better among perennials and annuals than among the "improved" large-flowered roses.

COLOURS AND COLOUR COMBINATIONS

There are perhaps few flowers which cause experts so much trouble in relation to colour combination as roses, and there is scarcely a single rose garden where a completely harmonious colour effect has been attained.

Even if the gardener used only a selection of the many fine roses available today, he would still find it almost impossible to arrange them in such a way that the colours would all harmonise when seen from any angle.

It is recommended that the colour-conscious, fastidious gardener should plant only one variety in each bed and have evergreen bushes forming a blending background to the beds. It also helps

large-flowered roses. I am sure there are many people who can immediately visualise the unsuitability of such combinations. It would be a good idea to test how the roses and the proposed perennials and annuals look together, by putting them together in a bunch. There is certainly no objection to putting well-spaced white lilies together with delicate pink large-flowered roses, or blue perennial asters with yellow roses, scabious with orange-yellow roses, *Gypsophila*, or elegant, flowering sprigs of *Thalictrum dipterocarpum* together with delicate, pink or dark red roses. Try this method yourself and note down all the possible combinations which look pleasing to you and put them into practice as attractive combinations when the time comes to plant a few roses in the perennial border or in beds of various annuals.

Finally, it will become obvious that a number of the attractive new floribunda roses are particularly suitable as neighbours for many perennials with blue or violet-blue flowers. This applies to varieties such as Concerto, Zambra, Lilli Marlene, Rimosa, Sarabande, Allgold, Rumba and Masquerade which, thanks to their pure, strong colours and compact flower-clusters

Rumba

Ena Harkness

enormously if a bush or a few perennials or annuals with blue or violet-blue flowers are planted in among the more dangerous colour combinations.

All varieties of rose do in fact look attractive – singly – but some varieties can totally destroy each other when planted in beds close together.

The worst result will occur in the red group, which in recent years has acquired new varieties with bright tomato-red or geranium-red colours (Baccara, Texas Centennial, Farandole, Sarabande, Zambra, etc.). These look unsuitable or even repulsive when seen together with the scarlet and purplish shades of red (Ena Harkness, Hanne, Crimson Glory, Champs-Elysées, etc.).

These two colour groups, the yellow-red and the purple-red, which also has a tendency to become slightly bluish-red when the flowers are fully open, should be planted as far apart from each other as possible, so that these two shades of red do not have the slightest chance of being seen together. The bright yellowish-reds can also be placed closest to the observer, in company with pure yellow and orange-yellow varieties.

The delicate, pure pink varieties are also very sensitive to neighbours of other colour groups, and they really only tolerate white and pale yellow, with a little violet-pink and pale blue in the perennials and annuals. In addition, plants with grey and silvery-white leaves are very suitable as a background (*Eleagnus, Santolina, Cerastium, Cineraria, Stachys lanata,* etc.).

Finally, a word of warning – purely from the point of view of colour – concerning the yellow-red varieties among the new, profusely flowering floribunda roses. Their colour effect is so audacious that if possible they should be planted completely apart, in a place where their rather bold colours cannot embarrass other roses. This applies to varieties such as Rumba, Circus, Goldilocks, Masquerade, etc.

THE BLUE ROSE

We now have both blue and violet varieties of rose. These are not artificially dyed with the help of chemicals, but are true colours which are the result of deliberate hybridisation. What therefore should be our attitude to such "new creations" of horticulture?

Danse des Sylphes

First, we can say that it is really not a bad tradition that roses should principally be red, pink, yellow and white, just as cornflowers should preferably be blue, sunflowers yellow and anemones white. Nature has unwritten laws for the colours of certain flowers and this appears to be a sound conception. Blue, violet and green roses (*R. viridiflora*) must definitely still be regarded as curiosities, and as such they should only be used with care in the beds of a rose garden.

Colour plate 42 shows an attractive violet rose, and it is certain that others with this special colour will soon be available. The deep reddish-purple rose, Blue Boy, was launched in 1958 by the great German firm of W. Kordes; it has the growth form of a moss rose. Blue Moon (Tantau 1964) is the truest blue we have, but even it has a tinge of violet.

Cut roses

A bouquet of cut roses requires proper care if it is to remain fresh and attractive. Now that we have described how to grow roses in the garden it will be appropriate to say something about the care of cut roses.

The first and foremost rule is that garden roses should be cut early in the morning or late at night – never in full sun during the middle of the day. Whether the roses have been collected in one's own garden or purchased at a florist, the first job is to remove the thorns from the stem for about a third of its length, and possibly also to clip a little off the bottom of each stem. After this, the ends of the stalks should be dipped into boiling water and held there for about 45 seconds.

The roses should then be wrapped, 5–7 stems or more at a time, in a piece of paper and placed in a pail of cold, fresh water, so that the water comes up to above halfway on the stalks. They should remain in this for about half an hour before being arranged in vases.

The vases should be very clean and the water should be kept clear by frequent changes. A short length should be cut off the stems each time the water is changed; the roses will keep longer if this is done under water.

The water will stay fresh longer if a small amount of vinegar (about 1 tablespoonful to 2 pints) is added, and the roses will last better if a similar amount of sugar is dissolved in the water. When placing the vase in a room, remember that cut roses do not tolerate draughts, extreme heat or direct sunshine.

It is not possible to give firm rules about the choice of vases – one might recall a couple of lines from Gustav Froding's poem, *Idealism and Realism*: ". . . and roses in a cracked jug are still always roses". In general, roses will look most attractive in quite simple vases without pronounced ornamentation or other decoration. A pewter jug or a copper vessel will often provide a splendid solution to the vase problem – and the roses keep well in them.

If it is difficult to arrange cut roses attractively in shallow jars or bowls, one can use a so-called "Fakir" holder or a piece of "Oasis", a strongly water-absorbent material, into which the roses can be stuck if the stems are cut off at an angle.

A large bouquet, consisting exclusively of perfect, well-developed roses with long, stiff stems and glossy, dark green foliage will always be a delight to look at when arranged attractively in a simple vase of glass or pottery. And a single, large-flowered, long-stemmed rose in a slender vase will also be a striking decoration in any room – and its scent will soon permeate the whole place.

Finally it should not be forgotton that roses will look attractive in good company, either with green foliage from other plants or with other flowers, but these must be selected with great care and with a critical eye.

Cut roses keep longer if a small piece of stem is cut off under the water before they are placed in vases.

Great care should be taken in choosing vases for cut roses. One can, for example, put a single, large, showy Grace de Monaco in a small, slender glass vase, or fill an old rococo tureen with old-fashioned, scented Provence and centifolia roses. A modern, square-sided glass can be used for specially selected long-stemmed roses such as Super Star, or a tall, very slender vase for climbers which hang gracefully.

Foliage which is particularly suitable for rose bouquets includes the slender stems of *Mahonia aquifolium*, a compact bush, whose slightly prickly, glossy, evergreen leaves look splendid with roses. The foliage of ordinary asparagus can also be used; this resembles the Asparagus Fern sold by florists. The leaves of many perennials are also useful in rose bouquets, for example, those of *Thalictrum, Astilbe, Eryngium, Polygonatum,* etc.

When other flowers, whether perennial or annual, are to be mixed with roses, they should always be light, graceful types – and as a rule only from the blue, violet, yellow and white parts of the spectrum. Red flowers will usually clash badly with red roses.

During recent years, it has become customary to use the white, perennial *Gypsophila* Bristol Fairy as an attractive foil for roses. The annual *Gypsophila elegans* Covent Garden Market is perhaps even more attractive and very easy to grow (the seeds should be sown at the beginning of May). Among other perennials suitable for this purpose are *Lythrum* Dropmore Purple, *Salvia nemorosa, Scabiosa* Moerheim Blue, *Aconitum* Sparks var., *Aster* Wunder von Stafa, White Ladies and *Delphinium* Capri.

There is an enormous range of annuals which are particularly suitable for inclusion in a bouquet of roses. Amongst these are *Verbena venosa, Rhodanthe, Cosmea, Salvia patens, Scabiosa* and *Nigella*.

Finally, roses look extremely well with lilies, but only with the white forms such as *Lilium candidum* and *Lilium regale*.

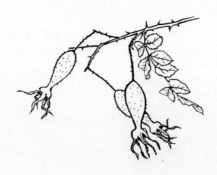

Choosing roses

After seeing the many colour plates of rose varieties and reading the descriptive text, the reader may perhaps be left with rather a confused impression of the whole subject.

The following lists are intended to be a help to the gardener who likes to choose his own roses. The selection is arranged in groups according to colour, scent and height.

The following abbreviations are used in the lists:

FL – Floribunda roses
CL – Climbing roses
SR – Shrub roses
HP – Hybrid perpetual
HT – Hybrid tea roses

SCENTED ROSES

Baronne Adolphe de Rothschild HP
Belle Blonde HT
Charles Bonnet HP
Christopher Stone HT
Chrysler Imperial HT
Columbine FL
Crimson Glory HT
Diamond Jubilee HT
Eden Rose HT
Etoile de Hollande HT
Général Jacqueminot HP
Gloire de Dijon CL
Grace de Monaco HT
Gruss an Zabern CL
Hanne HT
Konrad Adenauer HT
Maigold CL
Mme Butterfly HT
Mrs John Laing HP
President Herbert Hoover HT
Sanders White CL
Iceberg FL
Super Star HT
Sutter's Gold HT
Zéphirine Drouhin CL

Selection of roses grouped according to colour.

WHITE VARIETIES

Edina HT
Frau Karl Druschki HP
Gruss an Zabern CL
Iceberg (Schneewittchen) FL
Innocence HT
Irene of Denmark FL
Message HT
Nevada SR
Sanders' White CL
Stella Polaris SR
Virgo HT
White Dorothy CL
Yvonne Rabier FC

PALE PINK VARIETIES

Ballet HT
Dainty Bess HT
Edith Nellie Perkins HT
Frühlingsmorgen SR
Grace de Monaco HT
Gruss an Aachen FL
Maiden's Blush SR
Märchenland FL
Margot Koster FL
Mevrouw Nathalie Nypels FL
Michèle Meilland HT
Mme Butterfly HT
Mme Caroline Testout HT
Mrs John Laing HP
New Dawn CL
Picture HT

Pink Grootendorst s r
Poulsen's Bedder (Poulsen's Grupperose) f l
Poulsen's Delight f l
Poulsen's Pink f l
Tiffany h t
Tivoli f l

DARK PINK VARIETIES

Aloha c l
American Pillar c l
Betty Prior f l
Betty Uprichard h t
Chaplin's Pink c l
Charles Bonnet h p
Dame Edith Helen h t
Dorothy Perkins c l
Eden Rose h t
Fru Dagmar Hastrup s r
Perfecta h t
Pink Peace h t
Queen Elizabeth f l
Tausendschön c l

RED VARIETIES

Within the red colour group there are great
variations, from orange-red, sealing-wax red,
glowing blood-red to dark, velvety purple-red,
and so it is always advisable to check the colour
first before planting it close to other red varieties.

Alain f l
Ama f l
Baccara h t
Blaze c l
Champs-Elysées h t
Christopher Stone h t
Chrysler Imperial h t
Concerto f l
Crimson Glory h t
Crimson Velvet h t
Danse de Feu c l
Danse des Sylphes c l
Elsinore f l
Ena Harkness h t
Etoile de Hollande h t
Excelsa c l

Farandole f l
F. J. Grootendorst s r
Frensham f l
Général Jacqueminot h p
Hanne h t
Heidelberg c l
Hiawatha c l
Jolie Madame h t
Josephine Bruce h t
Konrad Adenauer h t
Korona f l
Lilli Marlene f l
Meteor f l
Paul's Scarlet Climber c l
Poinsettia h t
Poppy f l
Rödhätte (Red Riding Hood) f l
Royal Scarlet c l
Super Star h t
Ulrich Brunner h p
Wilhelm Hansman c l

ORANGE-RED VARIETIES
(also two-coloured – red and yellow, etc.)

Circus (yellow and pink and pure red) f l
Columbine (pale yellow flushed red) f l
Fashion (coral peach) f l
Grande Duchesse Charlotte h t
Masquerade (yellow and pink and red) f l
Mojave h t
Montezuma h t
Mrs Sam McGredy h t
Orange Triumph (pure red-orange) f l
Piccadilly (scarlet and yellow) h t
President Herbert Hoover (yellow and red) h t
Rumba (red and yellow) f l
Sarabande (orange—scarlet) f l
Soraya h t
Spartan f l
Suspense (red and yellow) h t
Talisman (red and yellow) h t
Texas Centennial h t
Toni Lander f l
Tzigane (red and yellow) h t
Zambra (orange and yellow) f l

YELLOW AND ORANGE-YELLOW VARIETIES

Allgold F L
Belle Blonde H T
Bettina H T
Buccaneer H T
Chinatown F L; S R
Climbing Goldilocks C L
Cynthia Brooke H T
Diamond Jubilee H T
Easlea's Golden Rambler C L
Flaming Sunset H T
Frühlingsgold S R
Geheimrat Duisberg H T
Golden Jewel F L
Golden Masterpiece H T
Golden Showers C L
Golden Sun H T
Goldilocks F L
Gloire de Dijon C L (yellow and pink)
Grand'mere Jenny H T
High Noon C L
Leverkusen C L
McGredy's Sunset H T
Maigold C L
Marcelle Gret H T
Mrs Pierre S. Dupont H T
Peace H T (yellow and pink)
Persian Yellow S R
Rimosa F L
Rosa Hugonis S R
Rustica S R
Spek's Yellow H T
Sutter's Gold H T (yellow and red)
Tawny Gold H T
Yellow Pinocchio F L

MISCELLANEOUS

Prelude (lavender) H T
Rose Gaujard (dark pink and white) H T
Sundance (pink with orange shading) F L
Veilchenblau (violet blue) C L

ROSES GROUPED ACCORDING TO HEIGHT

This list includes some of the best varieties but it does not contain all those shown in the colour plates. The heights given must be taken with a little reservation as these may vary according to the soil and the degree of pruning.

LOW ROSES

(about knee height, ca. 24 inches)

Allgold F L
Concerto F L
Cricri (miniature rose)
Goldilocks F L
Gruss an Aachen F L
Geheimrat Duisberg H T
Farandole F L
Flaming Sunset H T
Lilli Marlene F L
Margot Koster F L
Message H T
Meteor F L
Mrs Pierre S. Dupont H T
Mevrouw Nathalie Nypels F L
Perla de Alcanada (miniature rose)
Rimosa F L
Rumba F L
Sarabande F L
Spartan F L

MEDIUM-SIZED ROSES

(about hip height, ca. 36 inches)

Alain F L
Ballet H T
Betty Uprichard H T
Champs Elysées H T
Chrysler Imperial H T
Ena Harkness H T
Golden Sun H T
Grace de Monaco H T
Hanne H T
Marcelle Gret H T
Michèle Meilland H T
Orange Triumph F L
Perfecta H T
Piccadilly H T
President Herbert Hoover H T
Rose Gaujard H T
Iceberg F L

Spek's Yellow HT
Super Star HT
Suspense HT
Tiffany HT

TALL ROSES

(about breast height, ca. 40 inches and over)

In addition to the large-flowered varieties listed below all the shrub roses depicted in colour plates 59–64 will grow to over 3 feet in height.

Charles Bonnet HP
Chinatown FL
Chrysler Imperial HT
Eden Rose HT
Frau Karl Druschki HP
Frensham FL
Korona FL
Mrs John Laing HP
Märchenland FL
Queen Elizabeth FL
Peace HT

ROSES WITH VERY LARGE, WELL-FILLED FLOWERS

Ballet HT
Belle Blonde HT
Champs-Elysées HT

Crimson Glory HT
Chrysler Imperial HT
Diamond Jubilee HT
Eden Rose HT
Ena Harkness HT
Grace de Monaco HT
Grand'mere Jenny HT
Konrad Adenauer HT
Peace HT
Perfecta HT
Pink Peace HT
Rose Gaujard HT
Tiffany HT

ROSES WITHOUT THORNS (almost)

Baccara HT
Charles Bonnet
Irene of Denmark FL
Michèle Meilland HT
Queen Elizabeth FL
Picture HT
President Herbert Hoover HT
Rosa rubrifolia SR
Spek's Yellow HT
Tausendschön CL
Veilchenblau CL
Virgo HT

Glossary

Basis The term usually used for the lowermost or innermost part of the flower itself.

Budding A method of propagation in which an "eye", or bud, from a rose shoot is inserted in a slit behind the bark of a wild stock. The bud then grows together with the stock, which is later cut off just above the propagation point (see drawing, p. 64).

Chromosome number The small rod-shaped bodies seen when a plant cell nucleus is examined under the microscope are called chromosomes. The number of chromosomes varies according to the genus, but it is constant, and divisible by 2, e.g. 14, 28, 48, etc., within the same plant species. When a cell divides, the chromosomes split lengthwise into two, and each half passes to one of the two newly formed cells; by this means the hereditary material is continually transmitted to the next generation. When the sex cells (stamen cells and ovules) are formed in the flower, each one receives only half of the number of chromosomes that is characteristic of the genus. At fertilisation their chromosomes unite to give the normal number, and if there has been cross-pollination, new hereditary material will be brought in.

Clone A general term for all the descendants arising by vegetative reproduction (cuttings, budding, division) from a single, selected and particularly valuable individual plant.

Diploid Cells in which the nuclei have a double number of chromosomes are said to be diploid. In contrast to this a cell with a single complement of chromosomes is haploid.

Dormant eye A horticultural term for those buds, sitting in the axils of leaves or shoots, which only start to develop if the shoot is pruned just above them.

Emasculation Removal of the male sexual organs or stamens from a rose flower, an operation performed in the hybridisation of roses.

Eye Both the true leaf and flower buds on a rose plant and the buds used for budding are called eyes.

Fertile Capable of fertilising, the opposite of sterile.

Generic name The Latin term, *Rosa*, is the generic name for all roses. The rose genus, together with, for example, the strawberry belongs to the rose family, or *Rosaceae*. See also under species name.

Habit The external characteristics and appearance, e.g. pendulous growth, very curved branches etc.

Heeling-in Temporary storage of plants in a pile of earth or in sphagnum moss until they can be properly planted.

Humus The brown or black constituent of the uppermost layer of soil, consisting mainly of organic compounds, resulting from the decay of plants and animals left behind in the soil.

Hybrid A plant produced by crossing or hybridising two selected varieties with the intention of combining in the new plant or hybrid one or more characteristics from the parents. Hybrids are by no means always successful, and much selection has to be carried out.

Mutation A sudden and unpredictable change in the organs and appearance of a plant. For instance, a rose bush with red flowers may suddenly produce a shoot bearing yellow flowers.

pH value The pH value denotes the content of hydrogen ions per unit volume of soil. Chemically pure water is neutral and this is said to have a pH of 7. If, for example, the amount of calcium carbonate increases, the pH value will rise. Very few plant species will be able to grow in a soil with a pH of 10 or over which is too alkaline. When the pH falls much below 7, as for example in moorland soil or sphagnum moss, which have a pH of 4–5, the soil is said to be acid or poor in calcium, and only a few plants will be able to thrive in it (acid-soil plants). It is always important to find out the soil pH before starting to plant and one should also know the pH at which a given plant thrives best. For growing roses the pH should be 5·5–7, that is, a little on the acid side. If the pH value is too high it can be lowered by the addition of peat-moss (sphagnum), or, for example, ammonium sulphate or sulphur.

Pollen The powder, formed on the stamens of the flower, which in pollination is transferred to the stigma. This can take place either within the same flower (self-pollination) or between two different flowers (cross-pollination).

Propagation point The place on the stock where the scion from the improved rose variety is budded or grafted, so that it grows together with the stock.

Remontant Rose varieties which flower two or more times in the course of a summer are said to be remontant (or hybrid perpetual).

Scion Term for that part of a plant, whether bud, branch or shoot, which is grafted or budded on to the stock.

Seedling A rose plant produced from a sown seed.

Soil analysis Chemical investigation of soil to find out its content of important nutrient substances, such as phosphorus, potassium, nitrogen etc. This is done, for instance, in the laboratories of horticultural societies. *See also pH value.*

Species name The Latin or scientific name of a plant consists of two parts – a generic name and a species name; among the roses there is usually also a name for the variety. Thus *Rosa eglanteria* Lucy Bertram is made up of a generic name *Rosa*, species name *eglanteria* and the variety name Lucy Bertram.

Sport A rose variety which arises suddenly and unexpectedly by reason of changes in the hereditary material. See also *mutation*.

Stock The wild stock or stem on to which another rose – an "improved" variety – is grafted or budded. The most commonly used stocks are *R. canina* and *R. rugosa*. Once the bud or graft has started to grow, the stock is cut off immediately above the point at which budding or grafting took place. In a garden rose, therefore, it is only the root which is "wild".

Sucker A shoot arising from the stock on which a selected rose is grafted or budded. Suckers must be removed completely so that they do not take strength away from the selected rose.

Varietal name A rose that has arisen from the hybridisation of two other rose varieties or species is usually given a varietal name. Thus in *R. eglanteria* Lucy Bertram, the last two words constitute the varietal name.

Variety A differing form of a species, produced artificially or arising from natural causes.

A variety produced by hybridisation or crossing is known as a hybrid, e.g. hybrid teas.

Bibliography

It would not be appropriate to give here any form of comprehensive list of books and other publications on roses, but the following selected titles should be useful. Besides being a source of inspiration, several have also been of great assistance and value in the preparation of this book. In addition, both the Royal National Rose Society and the American Rose Society produce annuals.

EDWARD A. BUNYARD, *Old Garden Roses*, London 1936
A fine, inspired description of the old garden roses – up to about 1840. It deals with the historical development throughout the ages and also gives detailed descriptions of the roses.

PETER COATS, *Roses*, London 1962
A popular and colourful history of rose cultivation and its place in art, literature and history.

H. EDLAND, *Roses in Colour*, London 1963
This useful handbook for every gardener has 421 rose varieties photographed in colour.

GORDON EDWARDS, *Roses for Enjoyment*, London 1962

F. FAIRBROTHER, *Roses*, London 1958; third revised edition 1965
An excellent little handbook in the Penguin series, produced in collaboration with the Royal Horticultural Society.
Illustrated Guide to Roses, London 1966

N. P. HARVEY, *Roses in Britain*, London 1951

W. KORDES, *Das Rosenbuch*, Hanover 1956
A beautifully illustrated book written for both amateur and expert by the well-known rose breeder.

J. H. MCFARLAND, *Modern Roses VI*, Harrisburg 1965
A profusely illustrated American handbook on modern garden roses.

EVA MANNERING, *The Best of Redouté's Roses*, London 1959
A large-format volume with very beautiful colour reproductions of Redouté's famous rose paintings.

A. NORMAN, *Successful Rose Growing*, London 1962

BERTRAM PARK, *Collins Guide to Roses*, London 1956; *The World of Roses*, London 1962

ROY E. SHEPHERD, *History of the Rose* and *Roses*, London 1954

A. S. THOMAS, *Better Roses*, London 1954

GRAHAM S. THOMAS, *The Old Shrub Rose*, London 1961; *Shrub Roses of Today*, London 1965

Index